W9-CBV-568

FreeMo
JOURNALS

In response to many requests for small group and Sunday school materials, Light and Life Publishing is pleased to present the FreeMo Journals. These books have been ideally prepared for any leader to facilitate discipleship in a small group setting, or for individual Christians to employ as a resource for their daily devotions.

The FreeMo Journals cover a wide variety of topics, but have been framed around the Free Methodist Church's Nine Strategies for whole church growth.

- Rev. Jay Cordova, Publisher, Free Methodist Church - USA

Design by Jake Blythe
Diagrams by Nicolle Kennelly

URBAN SHALOM

RESTORING HOPE AND JUSTICE TO GLOBAL COMMUNITIES AFFECTED BY MODERN SLAVERY

BY DR. KEVIN AUSTIN WITH KATIE BERGMAN

CONTENTS

FOREWORD

As followers of Jesus we delight in the good news that our Savior God hears the cries of those groaning in slavery and moves in saving ways to rescue. Time and again our story–God's story–recounts how God saw the bondage of a people and provided a way out–an Exodus, and then a way into a life of promise where people thrive.

Of course, the story of Moses comes immediately to mind, but long before Moses' time the Lord God demonstrated a commitment to free captives and then use them to free others. Joseph became captive to the jealousy and hatred of his brothers, then to Midian merchants on their way to Egypt, then to a prominent Egyptian named Potiphar, and finally to confinement in Pharaoh's prison. At the last, God rescued Joseph from prison so that through him a plan could be worked to save not only Joseph's people, but all peoples. Long before the Hebrews became slaves in Egypt, their God had repeatedly responded to captive peoples by setting them free. Thus, the story unfolds as an up and down, back and forth saga of slavery and freedom of varying kinds until the time was right for Jesus the Messiah to announce the aims of his Spirit-anointed mission:

"The Spirit of the Lord is upon me, because he has anointed me to bring good news to the poor. He has sent me to proclaim release to the captives and recovery of sight to the blind, to let the oppressed go free, to proclaim the year of the Lord's favor."
(Lk. 4:18-19, NRSV)

In pursuit of that very mission, Jesus served, taught, healed, and invited any who wished to live in the freedom of God's kingdom. Many rejoiced and were set free, but offering freedom was not without consequences. Indeed, Jesus suffered misunderstanding, opposition, slander, betrayal, denials, accusations, and finally arrest, conviction, and execution. All for freedom–which burst powerfully onto the human scene on the third day in the most astounding way, as the most fearsome form of bondage–to death itself–surrendered to a freedom birthed out of Jesus' loving sacrifice.

Shortly after that third day, the first waves of Jesus' freedom movement formed and fanned out across the then known world. Wherever the Jesus-people went they called people from death to life, from darkness to light, and from slavery to liberty. Just a few years later, the Apostle Paul put it like this to one of his churches: it was for freedom that the Messiah set you free. So, stand firmly in that freedom and use it to love one another and the world (see Gal. 5:1 ff.). In all the centuries that have followed, Jesus' followers have been most true to their identity and calling when they have joined Jesus in setting people free.

It is natural, therefore–we might say "it is in our DNA"–to be broken-hearted over the plight of millions of people who live today enslaved in some way, many of whom are women and children. It is natural for us to say "NO!" to the powers and systems that design or support such slavery. And it is a matter of sacred calling to join with as many as possible in setting people free.

For several years, now, the Free Methodist Church - USA has put hands and feet into responding to the scandalous modern reality of the human slave trade in all its forms. Across the country churches have become educated, impassioned and activated in practical ways that contribute to a growing movement of abolitionists who share God's concern for setting people free.

Dr. Kevin Austin is one of my heroes in this regard. It was he who first called his denomination to deepened awareness of the scourge of human trafficking. He wrote a powerful proposal for his church to engage in this fight and then was commissioned as the first missionary assigned to a cause. But for Kevin and the scores of others he has enlisted, this is not just a cause. It is a matter of sacred vocation, and not only for some of God's people but for all of them. In the pages that follow you will feel his passion, learn what communities of Jesus' followers can do to help free modern slaves, and be inspired to live in the direction and for the sake of freedom for all people.

David W. Kendall, Bishop
Free Methodist Church-USA.

INTRODUCTION

I remember the first encounter I had with what I now know as modern slavery.

I was on my first short-term missions trip to Cambodia. During the day I taught pastors, but the evenings were spent playing with children at the nearby International Child Care Center's House of Love, as well as in lively conversations with the Filipino missionary, Paula Guazon. A few days into our time together Paula was visibly upset. One of the children from the House of Love had been sold to a Japanese couple in Phnom Penh to be a domestic helper. I vividly remember agonizing with her, wondering how this could happen. I didn't know it at the time, but this happens regularly across the globe.

My second real encounter was with a young, Thai woman, whom I call "Gung."

Gung was a close personal friend of our family. She spent a lot of time with us. One evening, she showed up at our home and tearfully related how her father had sold her as a child from man to man as they moved from construction site to construction site. Our hearts broke with hers. We began to understand why she had always engaged in a troubling pattern of behavior of attending church, then disappearing for a few months, and then returning repentant. At first we didn't know what was happening. What we learned was that she would meet a young man, with whom she would "hook up" and live together while ceasing to attend church. But after they broke up she would return and try to put her life back together again. She did this over and over.

We had always encouraged her to stop this behavior, to no effect, not knowing this young woman was sexually abused thousands of times as a child. It confused her about love and sex, forever changing her pattern of relationships with men. But that evening when she shared her story, and we wept and lamented with her, God started to work like never before.

This broke me. It continues to break me. From Illinois to India, in Seattle and Bangkok, affecting the Roma in Bulgaria and the poor in Ethiopia–in every country there are countless stories of abuse and oppression. Similar to homelessness, wealth disparity, and other issues, human trafficking often thrives in urban centers, from Atlanta to Amsterdam to Addis Ababa.

The more I've seen of human trafficking, or modern slavery, the more I've become convinced that it's actually a symptom of a much deeper problem. The real problem is brokenness. We've moved away from caring for each other in community, and we don't know how to live together any longer. As a result communities are broken, too. This spills out into broken systems and cultures. This community breakdown creates a breeding ground for not only exploitation and slavery, but it also perpetuates poverty, racism, gender inequality, and other injustices.

But there is hope. Jesus has been anointed to proclaim good news for those who need it, liberty for the captives, healing for the broken, the jubilee arriving for God's people. (Luke 4:16-21) Jesus liberates, saves, and brings healing and hope. We are invited not only to be free, but also to thrive in the new future, and then to partner with God to set others free in the name of Jesus.

That's why we can't talk about slavery without talking about our mutual brokenness–in both parishioners and pastors, in pupils and teachers, in service recipients and service providers–and how God longs to frees us all. Only Jesus can liberate us and heal us. Once we are liberated we join with others on the journey of following Jesus toward shalom.

What does it truly mean to be set free and live in the freedom Jesus offers? Is it physical, emotional, mental, and/or spiritual? How does it manifest in our lives personally? What is our role in helping set others free? These are the questions we will unpack and explore together in this book.

The kind of freedom we're discussing is not just manumission, but liberation. Manumission is being set free, released from bondage. Liberation is to be set free with rights and responsibilities of citizenship. The former is only release from something. The latter is to be given a new future. It is physical, emotional, mental, and spiritual. It is personal, but also communal.

Where do we start? As people of faith we start with God. Liberation is God's doing, not ours–though we do respond. God has a mission and we partner with God. In doing this, it's tempting to start with the problem and then leap into seeking solutions. We must resist this. Solving problems is only a beginning. The real goal is transformation.

How we seek this transformation is as important as what we do. We believe a just process leads to a just outcome. The best actions flow out of character and community, informed and formed by the Spirit, the scriptures, and the person and work of Jesus.

Freedom. Discipleship. Hope.

Gung, our young Thai friend, wept as she told us of the sin that abused her as a child. We wrapped our arms around her and joined in her weeping. Together, we prayed. From that moment on there was a change. The sin broke, the shame started to heal. She became liberated, and together we were standing on holy ground. Years later there is still evidence of this change.

SECTION 1

FOUNDATIONS

CHAPTER 1

THE MISSION OF GOD

> They will enter Zion with singing; everlasting joy will crown their heads. Gladness and joy will overtake them, and sorrow and sighing will flee away.
> **Isaiah 35:10**

In the Kingdom of Thailand, despite the last 200 years of work by missionaries, Christians make up less than 1% of the population. As one of these missionaries to Thailand, I've come to see that one of the reasons Christianity has failed to take root is in our approach. We've mostly aimed at planting Western-style churches instead of focusing on advancing the mission of God, which transcends cultures. We've tended to emphasize the organization over and above relationships while sidelining justice ministries.

Thailand is also a place where slavery thrives in many forms. The most lucrative business in the Kingdom of Thailand is sex tourism.[1] This is clearly seen in places like Bangkok, where central areas such as Patpong are overrun with strip clubs and bars. Pornography and sex toys are for sale everywhere. In neighborhood after neighborhood, clubs associated with various countries are easily found in order to serve the international tourist. And Patpong is only one of countless hotspots where prostitution and sex trafficking flourish in Bangkok.

Bangkok, a hurting and broken city of more than 8 million people, is the kind of urban context where we need to engage and seek holistic freedom. Desperate people move to the cities looking for work. Entrepreneurs of an unholy kind are looking for ways to take advantage of the vulnerable. There is more opportunity for some in the city, but also more danger.

SHALOM

The mission of God and the mission of the church ought not be reduced to personal salvation, or programs to help others be set free, or evangelism, or church planting. These are necessary, but incomplete. The mission of God encompasses much more than these.

One word in particular gives us a good idea of what the mission of God is: shalom. At its core, shalom is about the flourishing of relationships that "dwell at peace with God, with self, with fellows, with nature."[2] It is grounded in justice and harmony within "an authentic and nurturing community in which one can be one's true self and give one's self away without becoming poor."[3] Most importantly, it is brought through Jesus.

Shalom is the ideal way of life that God intended and still intends. It is rooted in covenant relationship and companionship with God and between all the people of God. Shalom is the end of the journey begun in reconciliation.[4] It is the end result of mission and evangelism, and is holistic salvation. Salvation means all of creation, all relationships, all systems healed.

Sin is what interferes with shalom. Sin is disease, not just a matter of the law but an infection affecting creation, relationships, and systems. It is a divorce. Through salvation, we are not only rescued from sin, but healed so that we can flourish under the glory of God. This is shalom.[5]

CONSIDER THIS:

What does shalom look like in your community?

We see these ideas clearly in passages like Jeremiah 29:4-7. Though all hope is gone and the enemy seems to have won, God calls the people to settle into the city, to work for the common good, to be shalom in a context of wickedness.

Think about how hard this advice is. Jeremiah is writing to a conquered people, instructing them to do what seems to be unimaginable: work for the common good with those who have created an uncommon wrong. This is powerfully prophetic, even in our day!

God's people do this by being God's presence through prayer, by practicing faith through action, serving with mercy, advocating for the powerless, and by proclaiming the good news. Jeremiah boldly calls people to faithfulness and hope, presenting an alternative consciousness for an alternate community.[6]

How we engage in this mission with God is important. The way we do this is through the community of God. God is a triune God: Father, Son, and Holy Spirit. There is full equality, glad submission, joyful intimacy, and mutual respect between the three in one.[7] God is a community. God's mission, therefore, has to be viewed within the context of relationships.

Community is the starting place for engaging in mission.

CONSIDER THIS:

Are you experiencing God's shalom in your life?

We can learn how to do this from the widow and Elisha in II Kings 4:1-7. The widow is desperate. She is in danger of losing her sons to a creditor who will turn them into slaves. The widow reaches out to Elisha, the man of God. What is his solution? Elisha involves the entire community, seeking the help of her neighbors to protect her sons. Justice is a community event and belongs to the local church.

The Mission of God then is this: a community (the Holy Trinity) inviting us, the community of the King, on a journey toward shalom. We aren't starting with us. We aren't starting with an analysis of problems then rushing to solutions. We are starting with God, the holy Trinity, a community. It begins with who God is, then who we are in God, then it moves to what we do. Even when we move into doing, the focus is still more on being. Existence and relationships come first. What we do flows from who we are.

CONSIDER THIS:

Do you put God first in your daily prayers and studies, or do you focus mainly on you and your needs?

Our age is enamored with "McDonald's activism." We want to name the problem, move swiftly to solutions, celebrate success, and then move on. We love the dramatic reward of confronting problems and claiming easy victories in Jesus name. We love ticking things off of a checklist. The problem with quick solutions is that they rarely solve long-term issues.

We see this often along the non-profit and church ministry landscape. Giving handouts to people who are homeless is more immediately gratifying than engaging in the long and sometimes overwhelming process of entering into a relationship to address why people are homeless in the first place. In the anti-trafficking sphere, governments and donors tend to give more preference to rescue operations than the less glamorous but equally important work of prevention, through building the economic, environmental, and social resilience of a community. We need food banks and shelters and rescue operations, but that is neither where we start nor end.

Being on mission with God is about being, then doing; action becoming a characteristic of who we are in God. The end result is to work holistically in partnership with God towards shalom. It's about hope, healing, flourishing, forgiveness, abundance, peace, salvation, reconciliation, and grace.

Freedom is lodged tightly in this foundational understanding. We can only be truly free in the joyful embrace of the Trinity, partnering with others, on mission with God, living, being, and doing in the direction of shalom.

CONSIDER THIS:

Are you experiencing community with the Holy Trinity?

Shalom, however, takes time. And it's not always easy to quantify. I wish I could say that slaves in Thailand are being freed every day through the work of the Set Free Movement—but this isn't the case. I wish I could say that the church in Thailand is starting to thrive—but it's barely hanging on. Fortunately, there are excellent organizations like Night Light Bangkok[8] that are rescuing and restoring victims of commercial sexual exploitation. Also, there are national leaders and missionaries in the Free Methodist church and other denominations doing excellent work. Even so, we don't always see the results we seek within the timeframe we want.

As we engage with God on mission, we need to remember we are helpers, not saviors. Let's think of ourselves as farmers: "Before we reap a harvest, we need to plant and water and let things grow in a healthy environment. We prepare the land. We prune the plant. We get our hands dirty. We make ourselves vitally aware of the threat of natural disasters, but we are not deterred by them. And most of all, we patiently wait."[9]

As we pursue shalom, we must have a posture of humility and a willingness to accept that God is bigger than any of our efforts.

QUESTIONS FOR FURTHER REFLECTION

How do you live on mission with God?

Does your church or group prefer to lean more towards doing or being? What about yourself?

How have you seen sin interfering with shalom in your own life, church, or community?

How have you seen "McDonald's activism" in your community? What might be the potential consequences?

What might be holding your church or group back from focusing more on who God is than on your church's personal mission?

ANNOTATIONS

1) Kevin Bales, *Disposable People*, London: University of California Press, 1999, 75.

2) Read Myer's book: Bryant L. Myers, *Walking With The Poor: Principles and Practices of Transformational Development* (Maryknoll: Orbis Books, 2011). Kindle Electronic Edition.

3) Ibid, location 1978.

4) Emmanuel Katongole and Chris Rice, *Reconciling All Things*, (Downers Grove: IVP Books, 2008) Kindle Electronic Edition, Locations 1233-1235.

5) Howard A. Snyder and Joel Scandrett, *Salvation Means Creation Healed: The Ecology of Sin and Grace: Overcoming the Divorce Between Earth and Heaven* (Eugene: Cascade Books, 2011), 108.

6) Walter Brueggemann, *Biblical Perspectives on Evangelism* (Nashville: Abingdon Press, 1993), 34.

7) See Seamond's book, *Ministry in the Image of God: The Trinitarian Shape of Christian Service*.

8) http://www.nightlightinternational.com/bangkok/

9) Katie Bergman, *When Justice Just Is*, (Bloomington: West Bow Press, 2015), 49.

CHAPTER 2

THE MISSION OF THE CHURCH

> So Jesus said to them again, "Peace be with you; as the Father has sent Me, I also send you."
> **John 20:21**

When we think about missions, our imagination often takes us immediately to an orphaned refugee from Syria or a drought-plagued village in Somalia or a hungry family in Haiti. But sometimes we neglect to include our own broken cities within the context of missions.

As I travel, I ask the same questions everywhere: what are the challenges in your community, and what are the opportunities? From small towns to big cities I hear almost always the same things: drugs are consuming our youth; systemic poverty is crushing families; racism and human trafficking are tearing our communities apart.

Many–if not all–of our cities in the U.S. are fertile grounds for missions. Our churches need to lead urban engagement if only for one reason: the children being exploited in every city across the nation.

There is a strong connection between commercial sexual exploitation and foster youth who haven't found a permanent, stable home environment in the U.S.[1] While the statistics vary from state to state and even city to city, anywhere between 50% and 90% of child victims of human trafficking were involved in the child welfare system at some point. In Connecticut, 86 out of the 88 child victims of sex trafficking reported in 2012 were in foster care.[2] In Florida, an estimated 70% of victims of human trafficking were foster youth,[3] while the number is slightly higher in New York City, at 75%.

How does this happen? Youth who "age out" of foster care at age 18 without ever finding a permanent home may end up vulnerable on the streets, without adequate economic or social support and are recruited into prostitution. Some run away from their foster families and are picked up by a trafficker within their first 24-48 hours on the streets. Others have endured intense trauma, which increases susceptibility to exploitation.

This is only one of many justice issues we face in the U.S. today. Where does the church fit in?

THE CHURCH'S MISSION IS GOD'S MISSION

In the previous chapter, we discussed the mission of God. So now, what about the mission of the church?

We often think that if we are following God we will be on mission with God. Sometimes we are. But sometimes we ignore God's mission because it's just too uncomfortable. Other times, we talk about the mission of the church as if it's a separate subject from God's work in the world. That's dangerous thinking.

Anglican clergyman and Old Testament scholar Christopher Wright stated: "It's not that God has a mission for the church in the world, but that God has a church for his mission in the world."[4] It's not about us, the church; it's about God and the mission of God. The church's activities, all that we do, are a means to the end, not the end itself. God is the subject and source of mission. The church is God's representative.

Think about it this way: imagine you are going on a family road trip, driving to the destination of your vacation. The car is important. It's necessary, in fact. But the vacation isn't about the car. The vacation is about being together on a vacation. Most of all, it's about what will happen at the end of the drive when you reach your destination.

When we focus on our mission, asking: "what should we do for God?" we turn inward. We start to limit the work of God to being about what we are passionate about: prayer, or social justice, or church planting, or evangelism—whatever draws our interest. Pride moves in when we think God's mission in the world depends on us. We feel a responsibility to fix all of the wrongs of the world. We start overworking. Programs and projects replace discipleship and community. And if our work is successful, more pride comes. It affirms that building relationships take too much time and that we're more effective when we try building God's kingdom with our own hands.

But the mission of the church is to be on mission with God. We don't need our own mission. God's mission is big enough for all.

CONSIDER THIS:

Do you view the service you do for God as acts primarily of obedience or relationship?

We need an expanded view of mission and evangelism. Mission and evangelism cannot be confined only to conformity to preaching Jesus' truths and engaging in simple actions like going forward to an altar. It runs deeper than agreeing to and confessing the truth. Conversion must go deeper to penetrate not just hearts and minds, but also families and communities, systems, and cultures. That's why creating change alone is not our ultimate goal; changing values and reshaping society is.

In Seattle, the First Free Methodist Church was deeply troubled by the exploitation and brokenness they were witnessing in their city and sought to partner with God on mission. Instead of starting with building a program, the church started with coming together as God's people. They formed a group–one of the early Set Free Movement teams–which gathered together for several years to pray and worship God.

Why is this so powerful? Because worship, properly defined, is about giving worth to something or someone. In other words: assigning a supreme value to something or someone. This, in turn, creates a value and values foster character. Like a healthy tree producing good fruit, good character produces righteous action. Worship is the context and the attitude out of which character and action grows, and worship is the starting point for the impartation of holiness. Worship forms and transforms not just individuals but entire communities. Most worship is done with others and therefore is a communal event, which unifies, directs, reminds, and focuses the worshipping community. Worship, moral purity, and justice are signs of a functioning biblical community.

CONSIDER THIS:

Does your church or community have a foundation of worship, moral purity, and justice?

In which areas could it grow?

Of course, we don't stop at worship. For our team in Seattle, their lengthy time of prayer and worship was as a catalyst for action. They moved to dialoguing with each other, their church, and their community about how exploitation was manifested in their community and how they could respond. When they saw a need to mobilize students, they helped launch the Set Free Movement student chapter at Seattle Pacific University. They explored existing local ministries, serving women who had been abused and volunteering with organizations addressing sex trafficking in Seattle. Today, they continue to do these things. But after several years of formation, exploration, and listening to God, they've been led to develop their own preventative strategy.

In their research and networking, the team learned about the pipeline of foster care children into exploitation. Local statistics for Seattle showed that an estimated 70% of youth who were sexually exploited commercially had been in the foster care system at some point. The team in Seattle started asking how they could help prevent these things from happening. They learned that there were no foster parent support groups in their community, so they volunteered to host monthly meetings, providing meals, foster parent training, and activities for the foster children in the community. The team also learned that children immediately entering the foster care system would sit alone in a child welfare office–sometimes all day or for days–while their social worker arranged a placement. The team sought to minimize that isolating and re-traumatizing experience by bringing the Office Moms & Dads program to their county to care for the children coming into foster care on an on-call basis. They also helped to furnish a child waiting room and provide each child with a care package of hygiene items, clothes, snacks, a flashlight, and a toy to get through their first 24 hours in care.

The outcome of their work is phenomenal. But what's equally significant is the process the church engaged in. They knew that being on mission with God means committing to three things: to a relationship with God, to relationships with others, and to having the heart of God, which leads to having God's values and joyful obedience. The church also didn't just pray and worship, and they didn't just act–there was a balance to the process. The worship and prayer formed and informed them and prepared them for the action to come. Empowered by the Holy Spirit, the team works for reconciliation, beginning first in being reconciled with God, then with each other.

We, too, must learn from the great physician, comforting and caring for the wounded while we ourselves are being healed. With humility we are being saved and offering salvation to others, forming passionate communities that point the way to shalom. Out of these freedom, joy, and grace flow.

QUESTIONS FOR FURTHER REFLECTION:

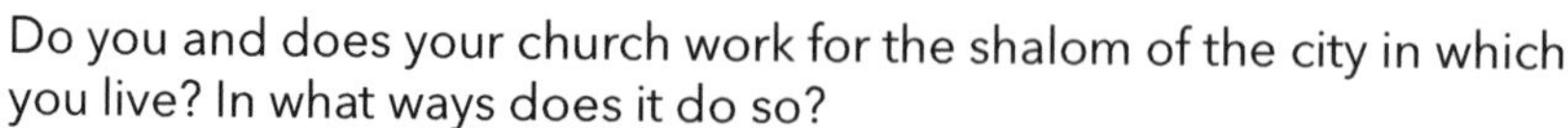

Do you and does your church work for the shalom of the city in which you live? In what ways does it do so?

Do you think you have a personal relationship with Christ? How does your personal faith fit within the larger context of the church community?

What do you think about expanding the view of mission(s) and evangelism? Do you agree? If so, why? If not, why not?

Do you agree with the statement that the church is a means to an end and not the end?

When thinking about foster care, how does your church care for children and youth who are vulnerable?

ANNOTATIONS

1) As many as an estimated 80% of men and women involved in prostitution in the United States were at one time in the foster care system. See: http://www.casre.org/our_children/fcht/and http://www.bettercarenetwork.org/sites/default/files/An%20Unholy%20Alliance%20-%20The%20Connection%20Between%20Foster%20Care%20and%20Human%20Trafficking.pdf

2) Connecticut Department of Children and Families "A Child Welfare Response to Domestic Minor Sex Trafficking" (2012). Available at http://www.ct.gov/dcf/lib/dcf/humantrafficing/pdf/response_to_domestic_minot_sex_trafficking.pdf

3) Vander Velde, Jessica. "FBI agent leads task force targeting pimps in child prostitution." *Tampa Bay Times* October 4, 2010.

4) Christopher J. H. Wright, *The Mission of God*, (Downers Grove: IVP Academic, 2006), 62.

CHAPTER 3

COMMUNITY AND FREEDOM

> But you are a chosen people, a royal priesthood, a holy nation, God's special possession, that you may declare the praises of him who called you out of darkness into his wonderful light.
> **I Peter 2:9**

As casually as possible, we watched the group of about twenty Filipino girls begin their after-school routine. The high school girls obediently worked on their homework while the younger ones played and danced to worship music. With such a joyful spirit in the air, it was hard to believe that each one of these girls had been sexually abused, sometimes even commercially.

Meeting these girls at First Love Ministries in the Philippines was sobering. It put faces to the problem we could no longer feel distant from: the growing epidemic of child trafficking. At least 100,000 children are trafficked into the sex trade each year in the Philippines, the majority of whom are girls between the ages of 14-17. Boys are also increasingly being trafficked and abused.

The Philippines is also a global hotspot for the online sexual exploitation of children, which is a billion-dollar industry. Human rights groups estimate the number of children involved specifically in live-streamed cybersex is in the tens of thousands.[1] As if that's not already hard to digest, we're learning that the victimization of these children often occurs in their homes by parents, relatives, and siblings. This is likely one of the most flagrant illustrations of how human trafficking starts with the breakdown of relationships.

Children in cybersex is only one of many complex forms of exploitation that thrives in the Philippines. An estimated 401,000 people live in forced labor and sexual slavery in the Philippines.[2] That's roughly the same size of the entire population of Nagasaki, Japan. Manila, the nation's capital, is a convenient place for international businessmen to purchase sex with children while traveling. Cities such as Sabang and Angeles City rest almost entirely on sex tourism to keep their economies afloat. From urban to rural areas, people are crying out for freedom, desperate for redemption.

THE EXODUS: FORMING THE COMMUNITY OF THE KING

Our brokenness, which began with Adam and Eve, expanded forward into all of history. The Bible is rife with examples of humans being objectified and then used or exploited. Sarai and Abram viewed Hagar not as a person, but as a means for paternity, a thing to be used (Genesis 16). Later Sarah is viewed as less than human, a thing to be taken by Abimelech. Abraham gives her away, motivated by the need for protection (Genesis 20). Jealousy and rivalry leads to Joseph being enslaved by his brothers, one of the earliest documented cases of human trafficking (Genesis 37:12-36). The entire nation of Israel becomes enslaved and cries to God to set them free.

It's troubling, and we can't ignore that God rarely condemns people who treat others unjustly in these stories. Perhaps God wants us to wrestle with these stories and form our own judgments. The behavior of these people is not admirable, and often neither is ours.

From the story of Joseph through Exodus 20, the long story of slavery becomes part of the DNA of God's people and the future church. Continually in the law and the prophets, God's people are challenged to remember: remember that they were once slaves in the land of Egypt; remember that God redeemed them. Freedom from slavery is the defining act of God for his people. This is no less true for Christians, since Jesus is crucified during Passover, the annual remembrance of freedom from slavery. While Moses begins the work, Jesus completes the work of freedom.

CONSIDER THIS:

Do you think of God's deliverance of the people of Israel as the defining work of God in both the Old and New Testaments?

God hears the cry of the captives. God sends a deliverer and stretches forth his hand of punishment on the slave owners and the oppressive system of slavery. God liberates his people.

The Exodus shows God's value for both freedom and community. The release of the captives is not just about political freedom. The liberation, journey, and new laws all point toward forming community. This new covenant community is characterized by the sanctity of human life and justice through their social and legal structures. Not just manumission, but liberation. Liberation is freedom with rights and responsibilities, full social and economic opportunities.

CONSIDER THIS:

Do you see yourself as emancipated or liberated? In what ways are you liberated, and in what ways might you not be?

This liberation and the surety of being under the leadership of God Almighty moved the people from a state of oppression and anxiety to a place of abundance and hope in a new community. In freedom the people could organize social power and social goods for the common benefit of the community. The Exodus provides the primary model of God's act of redemption, not just in the Old Testament, but also in the person and work of Jesus.

Israel is God's special possession, the community of the King. The Ten Commandments were given to preserve the community, and these commandments are a covenant treaty between a king and his people. God liberates and cannot be limited by systems and ideologies. God's sovereignty is not about arbitrary power, but about relationship with the community. God is the redeemer. In Hebrew the word for redeemer, gō'ēl, is a kinsman protector, a family member who is powerful and works to protect the family.[3] The Exodus must be seen then as action based on relationship.

Divine compassion leads to divine action.

The Sinai covenant is different from the preceding covenants. With Noah and Abraham, God's covenants are absolute and unconditional: God will act, preserve, bless, and protect. However, with the Sinai covenant there are conditions. The liberation is unconditional, but liberation only brings the Israelites to the wilderness. Once at Sinai the people are given the law, a covenant treaty with conditions, responsibilities, curses, and blessings.[4] This covenant treaty does not impose an ethical system; it exposes an ethical system, which is for the benefit of the people.[5]

God effected real change, a total response for a total need. Not only political or spiritual, not only physical, social, or economic—all of these. Lying, stealing, committing adultery, and exploiting others are symptoms of a broken community. The opposite, moral purity, is a sign of a functional covenant community. The covenant requires commitment and demands that the people act, as God requires. It's not just belief, but action based on beliefs. And it's not just actions and beliefs, but community with both God and each other.

CONSIDER THIS:

Do you feel that God is able to provide total freedom for your total need?

What might this look like in a contemporary context? With the human trafficking crisis in the Philippines, it's clear that change needs to come from the systemic macro level: Legislation needs to better protect children. The judicial system needs to be strengthened to more effectively prosecute perpetrators and bring closure for victims. Families need better access to education and secure employment. Droves of child-welfare professionals, foster care parents, and services for boys and male victims are needed. All of these are important–but they don't address the root cause of exploitation: the brokenness of community.

Children who are sexually exploited online are four times more likely to come from homes with poverty, addictions, neglect, and domestic violence.[6] These are more than injustices–they are sins. So while change must come through legal, economic, and social welfare systems, real transformation will come from the most basic level of human connection and values. Relationships in families and communities need reconciliation. Value systems that fuel exploitation need to shift so that humans are loved instead of used. People–exploiters, too–need to be taught that they are the precious children of God; that even when they are caught in the cycle of wrongdoings and shame, they are always within reach of grace and healing.

April Kenneth Joy Baldo ("Ken"), our Set Free Movement leader in Manila, the Philippines, is doing this in powerful ways within the urban context. Manila is an overpopulated, polluted city with many problems, but Jesus is present in Ken, radiating through all she is and does. She follows Jesus into the broken places because she believes she is on mission with God and is a member of the community of the King. She's working towards changing harmful systems that allow exploitation to thrive, but her focus starts at the relational level: investing in youth who will one day be leaders in the justice movement, equipping pastors to protect their congregations and communities from exploitation, helping parents see that creating a loving and safe space for their children is building their resilience against exploitation.

Like other Set Free leaders around the world, Ken has a palpable joy. She has been liberated and sees God stretching forth his hand to liberate all people everywhere, too. Eagerly, she partners with God and others to bring healing to her city and country.

QUESTIONS FOR FURTHER REFLECTION:

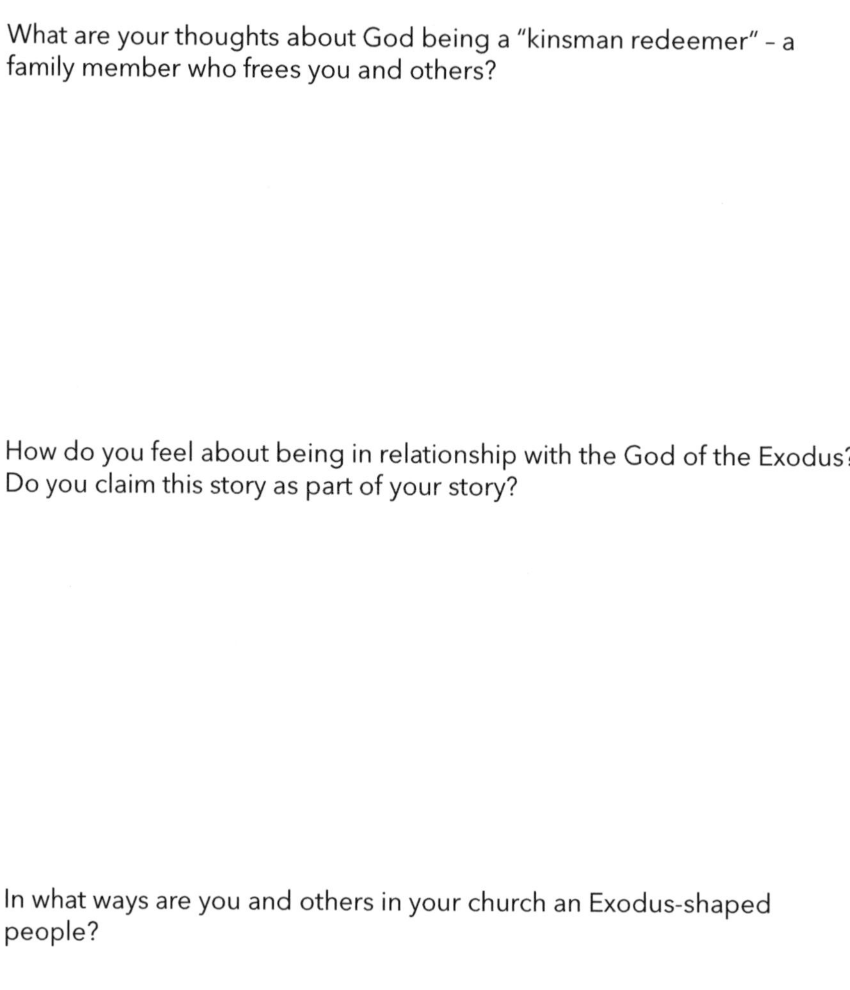

What are your thoughts about God being a "kinsman redeemer" - a family member who frees you and others?

How do you feel about being in relationship with the God of the Exodus? Do you claim this story as part of your story?

In what ways are you and others in your church an Exodus-shaped people?

How do you and how does your church view justice? Is it an essential part of the gospel or a distraction?

How do you find that safe space for discipleship, or how have you created safe spaces for others?

ANNOTATIONS

1) http://www.dw.com/en/the-philippines-booming-cybersex-industry/a-19026632

2) http://www.globalslaveryindex.org/country/philippines/

3) Christopher J. H. Wright, *The Mission of God* (Downers Grove: IVP Academic, 2006), 266ff.

4) Ibid, 77-78.

5) E. Stanely Jones, *The Unshakable Kingdom and the Unchanging Person* (Nashville: Abingdon, 1972), 146.

6) See page 48 of https://www.terredeshommes.nl/sites/tdh/files/uploads/research_report_2.pdf

SECTION 2

HOW DID WE GET HERE?

CHAPTER 4

SIN AND SHAME

> All day long my dishonor is before me and my humiliation has overwhelmed me.
> **Psalm 44:15**

In a crowded courtroom in Franklin County, Ohio, women of all ages and ethnicities gather as they do every Thursday. Despite their diversity, they have something in common: they're all emerging from human trafficking and exploitative situations. All of them have been convicted of various misdemeanors. All of them are recovering from drug addictions. All of them come from abusive homes and suffered early childhood trauma.

The specialized program they're participating in, called CATCH Court,[1] is based on a redemptive platform: that these women are in need of help and deserving of a second chance. Their lives have been marred by sin done by them and to them, but they are so much more than their sin. This community in Franklin County is founded on the belief that each person's journey begins not with original sin, but with original blessing. Each person is deserving of love, grace, and healing. Each one may be broken, but they are children of God first and foremost.

CATCH Court provides all the tools and means necessary for victims to escape the vicious cycle of abuse: housing, trauma-based counseling, clothing, medical care, and other forms of support that are key to their recovery. But perhaps even more important is the way these women are taught that they are loveable and worthy.

Most–if not all–of the participants have bought into the enemy's lie that because they've done bad, they ARE bad. But as they hear these truths–that God has called them out of darkness into his wonderful light–and invite the work of Jesus into their hearts, something changes. They are able to move from a place of feeling worthless to finding dignity. That's where hearts soften and shame can be shed, where relationships can be reconciled, where deferred dreams can be re-ignited, where harmful behaviors shift into healthy ones. That's where healing starts.

Injustices, the result of sin, are rooted in the breakdown of community. The evil power of sin seeks to destroy all relationships.

This started with the Fall, when domination became the norm. Adam subjugated Eve; Cain killed Abel; wars have raged. Instead of being godly, Adam and Eve sought to be God-like. They became usurpers. The original family's sin has infected all of their children.

The fall is not just about the sin of disobedience, a legal diagnosis. Sin is a disease and this disease creates broken relationships. For Orthodox Christians the fall is less about sin than about the loss of the presence of God. With disobedience came the breaking of community between God and the first family. To be a Christian, then, is not just to be forgiven, but to be recreated and to have the presence of God operational in our lives again.

Sin is not just a wrong choice. Sin is aligning with an evil power. Personal sin and social sin are a seamless package. Sin infects people and people operate within systems and cultures, so our systems and cultures become corrupt, creating the conditions in places like Franklin County, Ohio, for exploitation, gangs, and addictions to thrive.

CONSIDER THIS:

How has sin seemed like a disease in your life?

Howard Snyder, a former professor, pastor, and missionary, writes about the broken relationship between God and God's people:

> Sin turned God's creatures into predators rather than partners. The self-centeredness introduced by sin means that God's creatures are now ready to sacrifice each other's well being in order to satisfy their own desires—even if that means harm or even death to the other. . . the essence of sin may not be pride so much as the desire and willingness to exalt oneself, or prefer oneself, over another.[2]

We see in Ezekiel 16:49 that sin is about more than moral failure or breaking an ethical code—it's about how we treat others and live in the world. This passage states that Sodom's sin was arrogance, being overfed, and having no concern for the poor. Interestingly, the prophet makes no mention of sexual sin. However, the absence of sexual sin does not mean the earlier story is untrue or that Ezekiel is making light of moral purity. Sexual sin—desire misplaced—is sin, but it is not more of a sin than gluttony, selfishness, or ignoring the poor. Injustice, whether active or passive, is sin.

CONSIDER THIS:

How have you or your church engaged in passive injustice?

Amos has much to say. People are selling others into slavery. They are trampling on the poor, abusing justice in the courts, seeking luxury and pleasure at the expense of others. Amos condemns this behavior and ties it to religious aspects: that worship includes justice.

Bryant Myers writes:

> Poverty is about relationships that don't work, that isolate, that abandon or devalue. Transformation must be about restoring relationships, just and right relationships with God, with self, with community, with the "other," and with the environment.[3]

When sin entered the world so, too, did shame. Sin is about doing wrong things. Shame is about being a wrong thing. Sin can be forgiven, but shame can only be healed. The sacrifice of Jesus brings both forgiveness and healing. Only God forgives sin, but we partner with God to bring healing to the broken world.

For the women of CATCH Court, the abuse done to them was sin that created deep shame. These women are in desperate need of healing, not only from the abuse done to them but for the shame burdening them, too. This healing begins with the support of fellow participants, mentors, and professionals who not only hold them accountable but encourage them. Thursday afternoons together in the courtroom are not just accountability and correction; they also offer a place of laughter, community, and hope. They are fertile grounds for discipleship, since "Jesus' love is grasped and lived only in community."[4]

CONSIDER THIS:

How do you feel about being a partner with God in bringing hope and healing to the world?

The creation of Adam and Eve was the beginning of true, authentic community in our world. Sin, exclusion and objectification, pride and subjugation, wrong choices and evil power, harmed the original community. Fortunately, Christ removes sin and renames, recreates, and renews community. Christ as the new Adam establishes a new community.

CONSIDER THIS:

Do you think of sin primarily as moral failure or as an attack on the community and the mission of God?

SAINTS, NOT SINNERS

Instead of focusing on sin, let's look at the opposite: holiness.

God is holy. God is pure and sinless, whole, set apart, completely other. But God in Jesus is also with us and—through the Spirit—within and among us. Holiness is wholeness, integrity of heart and life. For John Wesley holiness is purity of heart, divine love. Holiness begins in relationship, becomes rooted in the heart, and flows into character and actions.[5]

Holiness is a way of life with a receptive side—our being—and an active side—our doing. God imparts his holiness and gives the Spirit to direct us, and then we respond in action.

Personal holiness is linked with social responsibility in Wesleyan theology. It's about "[finding] one's role in the building of shalom, the re-webbing of God, humanity, and all of creation in justice, harmony, fulfillments and delight."[6] Our personal holiness becomes a social holiness, rooted in community on our journey of sanctification. Sanctification is "conduct in motion."[7]

CONSIDER THIS:

Do you think of holiness and sanctification in terms of conduct in motion as a result of discipleship or in terms of rules?

Have you ever noticed that in almost all of the Pastoral Epistles the authors begin the letters with the salutation to "The Saints"? The people of Corinth were messed up, but Paul refers to them as the "Saints in Corinth." Their title, who they are, is not based on what they do or don't do. Behavior is important, but behavior doesn't determine our standing with God. God views us as his children, called and made holy in Christ. In this sense we are no longer sinners.

Do we sin? Yes. But the title only belongs to those before Christ. Once a person comes to Christ and follows him, the title changes from sinner to saint. We are saints. We are not dirty-rotten-no-good-sinners who can't do anything. That's a lie from the enemy.

I Peter 2: 9-10 states:

> But you are a chosen people,
> a royal priesthood,
> a holy nation,
> God's special possession,
> that you may declare the praises of him who called you
> out of darkness into his wonderful light.
> Once you were not a people,
> but now you are the people of God;
> once you had not received mercy,
> but now you have received mercy.

What a glorious identity we have in Christ! We are not powerless. We are called, chosen, gifted, able to do all that needs to be done, God being our helper. What's the only thing that stops us? Ourselves.

Freedom starts here. We are forgiven. We are being healed. We are partners with God. We are a holy people, on mission with God, bringing hope and healing to the world. Filled with the Spirit, we move forward in confidence, following Jesus to shalom.

QUESTIONS FOR FURTHER REFLECTION:

How do you view sin? For you is it primarily moral failure or an evil that seeks to destroy community? Do you believe that injustice is sin? Why, why not?

Is the notion that Jesus came not just to free us from sin, but also to heal our shame a new concept for you? What do you think? Do you feel you are being healed?

How do you experience the presence of God in your life?

How do you live into your calling as a holy people, called, gifted, and chosen?

Do you view yourself primarily as a sinner or a saint?

ANNOTATIONS

1) https://www.catchcourt.org/

2) Howard A. Snyder and Joel Scandrett, *Salvation Means Creation Healed: The Ecology of Sin and Grace: Overcoming the Divorce Between Earth and Heaven* (Eugene: Cascade Books, 2011), 101.

3) Bryant L. Myers, *Walking With The Poor: Principles and Practices of Transformational Development* (Maryknoll: Orbis Books, 2011) Kindle Electronic Edition, Locations 1988-1990.

4) Bishop David Kendall in Kevin W. Mannoia and Don Thosen, eds. *The Holiness Manifesto*. (Grand Rapids: Eerdmans, 2008), 69.

5) John Wesley, Sermon 24 in *Kinghorn, Vol. II, 21-33,* 116.

6) Cornelius Plantinga. *Not the Way it's Suppose to be: A Breviary of Sin* (Grand Rapids: Eerdmans, 1995), 197.

7) SPU *Holiness*, 11.

CHAPTER 5

THE NEED FOR JUSTICE AND FREEDOM

> This is what the LORD says: "Maintain justice and do what is right, for my salvation is close at hand and my righteousness will soon be revealed."
> **Isaiah 56:1**

Imagine a couple—let's call them Phil and Andrea—who attend your church. They've been heralded as some of the most active and virtuous members of your church for over a decade. They teach Sunday school, jointly lead the Monday night prayer gathering, lead Bible studies and prayer events, and help host an interdenominational conference on evangelism for their community every September. Nobody attends your church more regularly, prays more loudly, or fasts more frequently than Phil and Andrea, for which the couple is regularly praised by your pastor—much to Phil and Andrea's delight.

Last Sunday, your pastor invited a survivor of sex trafficking to speak to the congregation during the sermon. Her story shocked the entire congregation, especially Phil and Andrea. The two of them came to the front of the church and prayed fervently over the survivor, asking God to convict and change the hearts of those who exploit others. They returned to their seats, brokenhearted for the survivor but visibly pleased with their holy example to the rest of the church.

You don't know Phil and Andrea outside of church, and would never guess that the couple is at each other's throats most of the time. They present a united front at church every Sunday but are in a shouting match as soon as they get into their car on the way home.

Much of their feuding is spurred by Phil's absence at home, given the long hours he puts in on the job. Phil works as a general manager for a large construction company that almost exclusively employs Mexican laborers. Even though he feels irritated at the language barriers and is constantly yelling at his employees to learn English, Phil knows the advantages outweigh the frustrations. He prefers Mexican workers because he can pay them below minimum wage with impunity, since most of his employees are undocumented and won't risk deportation by complaining or reporting him. Phil regards himself as somewhat of a philanthropist by "helping these people out", providing on-site housing for the workers–even if seven or eight of them are crammed into one small trailer.

While Phil considers his actions to be business savvy, the Prophets would consider it to be exploitative. Taking advantage of the vulnerability of others is the kind of behavior that Amos and Isaiah condemn. Outside of the spiritual realm, labor exploitation violates the law and might be considered a criminal offence, even potentially a case of human trafficking.

Andrea, however, supports Phil's actions. One of the few things she and Phil can agree upon these days is being economical. As a stay-at-home parent, Andrea deems bargain hunting to be good stewardship and part of her responsibility. She's proud of herself when she scores a pair of half-price Skechers running shoes or stocks up on Black Friday sales for her kids at H&M. Even a bag of half-price Hershey bars gives Andrea a sense of accomplishment. Although she's seen the stream of Facebook posts with articles condemning these kinds of companies for their poor ethical standards and use of child labor, she figures it's not her problem. Her priority is the price tag.

Andrea's behavior may not seem particularly extreme. However, her preference for knowingly buying cheap goods from companies that are infamous for using slave labor makes her just as culpable as her husband. Both Andrea and Phil are funding modern slavery while passing it off as resourcefulness. They publicly oppose the issue of sex trafficking, but fail to see their connection to fuelling labor trafficking. They make an outward commitment as servants of God, but directly and indirectly abuse God's people–for lower business costs and cheap chocolate bars.

HEART BEFORE ACTION

The church has never been exempt from inconsistencies between belief and practice. We see this in the first chapter of Isaiah, where the prophet is furious with Israel's leaders for perverting justice and with the people for their ingratitude and corruption. In 1:17 the prophet gives us five action verbs and connects the proposed action in v. 18 with righteousness and forgiveness of sin:

> LEARN to do right,
> SEEK justice,
> DEFEND the oppressed,
> TAKE UP THE CAUSE of the fatherless, and
> PLEAD THE CASE of the widow.
>
> Come let us reason together,
> Though your sins are like scarlet,
> They shall be white as snow.

In Isaiah's theology what we do, how we care for the vulnerable and oppressed, is connected to either our sin or our salvation. This is not a "works righteousness." Isaiah is not suggesting that we earn our salvation by good deeds. He is showing that there is a logical, righteous connection between our rightness with God and also others.

Isaiah 58 is clearer still. The people are going through the motions. They are doing the right things: praying, fasting, and seeking God. However, their hearts are not right. They are oppressing their workers and quarreling.

CONSIDER THIS:

Do you sometimes just go through the motions in your relationship with God?

Like Ezekiel redefining sin, as mentioned in the chapter above, Isaiah redefines fasting as more than going without food, praying, covering oneself in ashes. True fasting is about having integrity with the heart of God, and this includes compassion and justice. True fasting is caring for the weak, the oppressed, the slave, the homeless, and other things.

Phil and Andrea, the fictionalized couple at the start of this chapter, are a contemporary example that HOW we do things is just as important as WHAT we do. Much like the people in Isaiah 58, Phil and Andrea have a compartmentalized spirituality. Outward appearances of godliness are more important to them than the state of their hearts. They present themselves as the quintessential Christian "power couple" but have a poisonous marriage. Their worship fails to include justice. Like many people, they are more drawn to the issue of sex trafficking–something they have no direct responsibility in–than labor exploitation, which they unconsciously fuel in their purchasing behaviors and the way they treat their employees.

And yet, we see in Isaiah 58 that purity begins with our character, not our actions. If our hearts and minds are in the right place, then righteous actions will follow. Then blessings will flow. God will be the rear guard, our guide, our healer, and will answer prayer. When we have the heart of God we will have the actions of God and the blessings of God.

What are we to make of these things?

First, the verses we've mentioned in this chapter are not just written to individuals, but to the community. All of us need to come clean, take up the cause, plead the case, fast with authenticity, feed the hungry, clothe the naked, set the captives free, and love deeply. We. All of us. Together. As Bethany Hoang writes,

> Justice is the work of community ... It cannot be pursued alone. Justice is a manifestation of Christ's body working at its very best ... Just as we need to intentionally open ourselves to God and God's leading, we need to open ourselves to doing justice in community. All of the body of Christ is called to be the Spirit-filled community that surrounds, supports, inhabits and propels the river of justice God is seeking to unleash ... And because every single member and role in Christ's body matters, it is critical that we learn to boldly discern what part of the body Christ has made each of us to inhabit.[1]

CONSIDER THIS:

Do you think of your spiritual journey as an individual endeavor or as a work of the community?

Second, these verses are to be read and lived out in the context of worship. Justice, as well as discipleship, and all we are, do, and think, is connected to worship.[2] If that's the case, then every pastor should have a track and field starting gun and at the last "amen!" of the service the gun is shot and everyone runs out of the church as fast as they can, giving away all the blessings they've received. Worship forms and transforms not just individuals but entire communities.

It's for this reason that the Free Methodist Church, the Church of the Nazarene, Church of God Anderson, The Wesleyan Church and others participate in Freedom Sunday, the last Sunday of September each year.[3] Freedom Sunday is a day when we purposely focus on the issue of modern slavery, and we worship in the direction of freedom. Worship is catalytic. It's the beginning, the middle, and the end of Christian social action.

Amos drives home these points. He confronts the neighboring countries and his people not only for idolatry, but also for the way people are trampling on the poor, abusing justice in the courts, turning people into slaves, and seeking luxury and pleasure at the expense of others. Amos demands that people repent and calls them to truly live, not just exist for personal pleasure. If you read Amos from The Message translation it will shake you:

> I can't stand your religious meetings.
> I'm fed up with your conferences and conventions.
> I want nothing to do with your religion projects,
> your pretentious slogans and goals.
> I'm sick of your fund-raising schemes,
> your public relations and image making.
> I've had all I can take of your noisy ego-music.
> When was the last time you sang to me?
> Do you know what I want?
> I want justice–oceans of it.
> I want fairness–rivers of it.
> That's what I want. That's all I want.
> **Amos 5:21-24**

Worship and justice cannot be divided. Both are equally divine. As Abraham Heschel writes, "What obtains between God and His people is not only a covenant of mutual obligations, but also a relationship of mutual concern. The message of God is not an impersonal accusation, but the utterance of a redeemer who is pained by the misdeeds, the thanklessness of those whom He has redeemed."[4]

Third, as mentioned in Chapter One above, we need to expand our view of mission and evangelism. Some see justice as a distraction from the "real" work of God: evangelism and church planting. But this reveals a skewed theology. It's not either/or: evangelism or justice, church growth or church health, self-preservation or self-denial, personal piety or engaged holiness. All are part of the mission of God. All are part of the calling of the church, but the priorities must be in the right order and the trajectory must be correct. Partnering with God and others to pursue justice is a sign that we get theology right.

Refuge Ministries, a chapter of the Set Free Movement in Wichita, Kansas, is an excellent example. Refuge creates intentional Christian community that addresses the hurts and needs of people who are homeless, hungry, unemployed, reintegrating from prison, or emerging from domestic violence, in order to prevent exploitation. The goal is not only spiritual and evangelical, or justice and compassion—it's shalom, which combines all of these. Discipleship, prayer, and church planting are as important to Refuge as its food pantry, homelessness outreach, and helping women reintegrating from prison to regain their dignity while meeting their basic needs.

The way Refuge shows compassion isn't transactional. It's not about the number of people fed or blankets distributed. It's about being the hands and feet of Jesus. Through a collaboration of churches, including Rivercrest Free Methodist and Northwest Free Methodist, each church takes turns hosting up to fourteen homeless people every night for a week. Church members feed them breakfast, a sack lunch, and a warm dinner. Members often play games with the children, help with homework, and build relationships with the parents. During the day, the parents can take showers, receive life skills training, and work with a case manager who helps them find a home and a job.

COMPELLED BY FREEDOM

"Freedom and obedience are both basic to the active life of holiness," argues John Webster, "because they direct us outwards, away from sinful self-regard and towards life in the truth of God's law." He goes on to explain how being sanctified by God makes us "consecrated for works of love" and compels us to "acknowledge my neighbor's cause and make it my own."[5]

CONSIDER THIS:

How do you view evangelism? What is it?

Knowing these things helps the church to think more holistically about its mission in the world. The mission of the church is to join with the mission of God. This includes proclaiming forgiveness of sins and working for the conversion of hearts and minds. It also means that we become agents of hope and healing in the world. We enter into God's redemption, cooperating with God, guided by the Holy Spirit.

CONSIDER THIS:

How does your local church help you think holistically about your journey with God and the mission of God?

This is why, as Christians, we cannot ignore the presence of slavery in our neighborhoods and around the world. Our own liberation should naturally propel us into service to help liberate others who are enslaved, whether through the slavery of addiction or mental illness or human trafficking.

The women living at Eden's Glory, a restoration home in Illinois, understand this. As survivors of human trafficking, all of them have endured the deepest and darkest forms of abuse but are on the journey to restoration. The freedom they are experiencing, the love they are receiving from staff and volunteers, and the grace of God that they are learning about is too beautiful to keep to themselves.

On one occasion, the residents at Eden's Glory met a homeless family in their community. When the women found out that the family needed money for a security deposit toward a place to live, their immediate reaction was missional. Using the gifts they had, the residents took to the kitchen to make baked goods and sold them in the community as a fundraiser to help the family.

Why? The residents empathized with the family because they knew what life is like on the streets. They, too, knew fear and uncertainty and poverty. But because of Christ's work through Eden's Glory, the residents also knew how powerful it is to have someone walk beside them as a presence of truth and fellowship. Being freed to a new life, these women, too, sought to free others.

QUESTIONS FOR FURTHER REFLECTION:

How is worship and the gathering of community catalytic?

What is your reaction when you read those words from Amos in 5:21-24?

Do you think of obedience and blessings as being connected?

How do you learn to do right, seek justice, and defend the oppressed?

Does your church participate in Freedom Sunday? Why? Why not? And what has been the result?

ANNOTATIONS

1) Bethany Hoang, *Deepening the Soul for Justice* (Downer's Grove: InterVarsity, 2012), 24-25.

2) Ibid., 36.

3) Find out more at https://setfreemovement.com/events/

4) Abrham J. Heschel, *The Prophets* (Peabody: Prince Press, 1999), 32.

5) John Webster, *Holiness* (Grand Rapids: Eerdmans, 2003), 96.

CHAPTER 6

FOLLOWING THE MESSIAH

> Jesus said to them again, "Peace to you! As the Father has sent Me, I also send you."
> **John 20:21**
>
> "But you will receive power when the Holy Spirit has come upon you, and you will be My witnesses in Jerusalem, in all Judea and Samaria, and to the ends of the earth."
> **Acts 1:8**

When you look at the official statistics of Bulgaria it's important to know that the Roma people who live within the borders literally do not count. The population statistics don't include them. There is extreme prejudice against the Roma. The Roma have a darker complexion, while the Bulgarians are light, which somehow justifies their marginalization.

In many cases, the Roma are completely unwelcome from joining mainstream society. In communities like Kyustendil, Bulgaria, the Roma live in a slum that is cut along a blunt line of racial discrimination, separating the Roma from the Bulgarians on the other side of town. Poverty rates are high while life expectancy and job opportunities are low. They are often denied access to health care and educational opportunities. The poverty and racism are crushing.

Some Roma families rejoice when a baby girl is born. They know that at some point in the future they can sell the girl and buy a horse for their transportation and work. In some cases, that girl is sold to an older man for marriage or ends up on the streets as a prostitute. There is a visible connection between racism, poverty, and exploitation.

How do we reconcile this–that a horse is worth more than a girl? That Bulgarians are considered to have more value than the Roma? How would Jesus respond?

THE MISSION OF JESUS

In the world of churches, non-profits, and businesses, we construct ourselves around mission or vision statements. A person asking *what's this organization about?* will usually first visit the website or annual report to read the organization's mission statement in order to get a thumbnail sketch of who they are.

The Free Methodist Church USA mission statement is:

> Love God
> Love People
> Make Disciples.

The Set Free Movement's mission statement is:

> We seek to end modern slavery and
> create new futures in
> partnership with others through
> community-based action.

At the beginning of Jesus ministry he entered the synagogue of his hometown and presented his mission statement:

> "The Spirit of the Lord is on me,
> because he has anointed me
> to proclaim good news to the poor.

> He has sent me to proclaim freedom for the prisoners
> and recovery of sight for the blind,
> to set the oppressed free,
> to proclaim the year of the Lord's favor."
> **Luke 4:18-19**

CONSIDER THIS:

What is the mission statement of your life?
What is the mission statement of your church?

There are four aspects of Jesus' mission that are significant. First, Jesus is able to make these statements and do what he did (and what he does today) by, through, and in collaboration with the Spirit of God. The Spirit of God was on Jesus. He, the Son of God, was anointed by the Holy Spirit. Think about that. Jesus was the Messiah–why did he need this anointing? If Jesus needed the Spirit, we certainly do as well. We can do nothing without the Spirit.

CONSIDER THIS:

How much do you rely on the Holy Spirit's anointing?

This circles back to some earlier observations: being proceeds doing. Jesus didn't come as a baby and as soon as he could walk started to heal, challenge, and teach. We have a brief story about how he learned in the temple, but beyond that we see a fully formed adult Jesus come to save the world. He was patient. He waited. He prepared in the desert. He humbled himself, even though he didn't need to, in baptism. Action came after formation.

Similarly, our strongest teams within the Set Free Movement emerge out of months or even years of praying and preparing themselves. Kelly Grace, our Set Free leader in Portland, Oregon, spent almost two years learning, praying, and networking. She invested in the time to be present in her community to identify the gaps, acknowledge its needs, and find like-minded partners before diving into strategy. What comes from this character forming approach is an informed, Spirit-led presence with resulting action.

Second, note how often the word "proclaim" is used. Jesus used words to announce the coming of the kingdom, the coming of jubilee. He didn't just act—he loved. He taught. He wasn't a human doing—he was fully a human being.

Non-profits and charitable organizations—even faith-based ones—often struggle to imitate this. Donors want to see tangible results and immediate outcomes. It's difficult for non-profits to measure the value of relationships, unity, and love. These things don't fit as well into annual reports and infographics. How can we support a shift in the way we seek justice to focus just as much on the being as the doing?

Third, note the things he is proclaiming: good news for the poor, freedom for prisoners, healing, liberation for captives, and then the favorable year of the Lord, the jubilee, when all debts are canceled. Like all mission statements there is much, much more than can be said about the work of Christ, but when we state that Jesus came to save the lost we have to include all of Luke 4:18-19 in the list of what Jesus came to do. Saving the lost is: freeing captives, partnering with God to be a healing force in the world, doing works of justice and mercy.

CONSIDER THIS:

How do you proclaim these things in words and deeds?

Again, we need to think holistically about the mission of God and the mission of the church. We need to be in harmony with what Jesus came to do. Jesus is the new Adam and brings us to shalom.

Finally, notice that his quoting from Isaiah 61 includes proclaiming the Lord's favor, but excludes "the day of God's vengeance." God is a judge. God will judge us on what we say, think, and do, but Jesus is not speaking here about the end of time–rather, the starting point of the year of Jubilee.

The intent of the Jubilee, found in Leviticus 25:8-13, is about the survival and welfare of families, but it is much more. Social justice is a focal point–not as charity, but as liberation, acclaiming God as sovereign ruler. The Jubilee is about "things God has created as they make their way back to the Father" or as a movement back to its source, a homecoming.[1] As noted above, freedom is liberation with rights and responsibilities, full social and economic opportunities; in other words, the recreation of community. God's reign and freedom go hand in hand.[2]

CONSIDER THIS:

In your life, do freedom and obedience to God go hand in hand?

God doesn't just free captives. God creates new futures. God frees people not just from something, but for something. God's people actively engage in works of justice, which bring hope and healing to communities, because they know that personal liberation is inseparable from helping others to be liberated. James Cone, an important African American theologian and activist, has much to say about this: because God has liberated the oppressed they now have a responsibility to join in the movement of God. "Reconciliation," he states, "is not only what God does in order to deliver oppressed people from captivity; it is also what oppressed people do in order to remain faithful to their new gift of freedom. Reconciliation is not just about justification, it is also sanctification and the new birth. Reconciliation, therefore, is not just one way, it is cooperant. Not just a freedom 'from' but a freedom 'for.'"[3]

The beginning of God's eschatological reign is marked by the proclamation of liberation and healing. Jesus was the herald and the center of this liberation. Jesus is not just an idea, a theology, a doctrine; and he's not even just a historical figure. Jesus is present wherever there is suffering and his presence sustains the oppressed and makes liberation possible.[4]

To be a follower of God, a Christian, Jesus is placed at the center of both the "being" and the "doing." Community and doing justice are not options; they are characteristics of the mission of God. To follow Jesus is not just to believe or attend church or "be saved," but to be radically transformed and a transforming presence in society.

LIBERATING THE OPPRESSED IN BULGARIA

Chance and Dee Dee Galloway, Free Methodist missionaries to Bulgaria, understand that to "know [Jesus] is to encounter him in the history of the weak and the helpless." [5]

On November 2, 2011, with only one piece of luggage per person, Chance and Dee Dee and their children left their home, jobs, and lives in Georgia and boarded a plane for their new home in Bulgaria. Years earlier, they'd taken several short mission trips to Bulgaria and felt deeply called by God to serve the Roma.

Chance and Dee Dee are living examples of Luke 4:18. They're proclaiming good news to the poor by discipling hundreds of adults and youth at the biblical training center they opened. They are proclaiming freedom for the prisoners by educating communities about human trafficking, which often preys on young Roma girls in the region who are sometimes sold into slavery for the price of a horse. They are setting the oppressed free by helping shift the harmful values that consider girls to be worth less than a horse in the first place. They are proclaiming the year of the Lord's favor as they mentor women, host youth camps, and plant churches.[6]

But these forms of outreach did not start on the day Chance and Dee Dee disembarked their plane from the United States. Humbly, they came to this community with no other agenda than to build relationships with the Roma as well as Bulgarian pastors and leaders. They balance relationships, discipleship, and justice as equally important.

They're not working simply to start projects in the community. They're there to help holistically transform it. And Jesus, the ultimate advocate of people in vulnerable situations, is present among them, guiding them on the path to liberation.

QUESTIONS FOR FURTHER REFLECTION:

What are you doing to love God, love people, and make disciples?

The Set Free Movement has a strong value in partnering with others. Do you partner with others to bring good news, help people live into freedom, etc.?

In your life, how do you interact with the mission of Jesus?

What are your thoughts about James Cone's statement that Jesus is not a doctrine or a proposition, but an event, and to know Jesus one must serve and help the oppressed?

How do you continually place Jesus in the center of your thoughts, words, and actions?

ANNOTATIONS

1) Ephraim Radner, *Leviticus* (Grand Rapids: Brazos Press, 2008), 265, 266, 262-278.

2) Sharon H. Ringe, *Jesus, Liberation, and the Biblical Jubilee* (Philadelphia: Fortress Press, 1985), 32.

3) James H. Cone, *God of the Oppressed* (Maryknoll: Orbis Books, 1975), 213.

4) Ibid, 30-34.

5) Ibid, 32.

6) Find out more at www.gallowayministries.org

CHAPTER 7

FREE METHODISTS HAVE "FREE" IN THE NAME FOR A REASON

> As the body without the spirit is dead, so faith without deeds is dead.
> **James 2:26**

> "Faith and works must go together. We must not only pray for righteousness to prevail, but do all we can in a Christian manner to make it prevail."[1]
> **BT Roberts**

Here's a trick question: should pastors go into brothels?

I asked this question to 600 congregants in Port-au-Prince, Haiti while the Bishop of Haiti was translating for me. He grunted, "No!" while his people looked puzzled.

Let me explain. In Mumbai, India there is a particular strategy law enforcement uses to raid brothels that use underage girls as prostitutes. Police require two witnesses to go into a brothel, create a transaction, while seeing with their own eyes that youth are being prostituted, and then walk out to tip the police. These same witnesses are needed months later to testify in court against the brothel owners. More than 400 pastors do this in Mumbai each year. Like actors in a movie, they take off their suits and ties and, wearing blue jeans and T-shirts, unshaven, sometimes with a pack of cigarettes in their pockets they go into the darkness to bring people into the light.

Our urban centers are places where injustices flourish. Jesus is in these broken places: the brothels, the slums, foster care offices, schools, on the streets, and in every home. He's calling us to come, sacrifice, and serve with hope and joy–sometimes in unconventional ways.

So, should pastors go into brothels? Yes, they should.

CONSIDER THIS:

Should church leaders go into brothels?

A HISTORY OF FREEDOM

After the deep dive of theology to this point, we now turn to the history of why Free Methodist pastors, leaders, and members are charged with the responsibility of seeking freedom.

The Free Methodist Church was birthed out of several central freedom-related issues in the 19th Century: the role of women in ministry, the nature of slavery, secret societies, and freedom of worship, just to name a few. Free Methodists spoke out against injustice and worked to change values in a way that would be inclusive of women, opposing of slavery, and focused on justice. In Western New York the emphasis was on free pews and freedom of the Spirit. In St. Louis "free" specifically meant freedom from slavery, and it was in this city that the first Free Methodist Church was formed.[2]

CONSIDER THIS:

How is your church or group working not just to fight injustice but to change values?

In 1899 there was a lively conversation in The Free Methodist weekly newspaper about whether or not to delete the Free Methodist stance against slavery from the Book of Discipline. On the one side, some saw keeping the language about slavery in the Book of Discipline as an obstacle to the gospel and a hindrance to planting churches in the south. Their reasoning was that since slavery was now legally abolished, the stance against slavery should be removed.

CONSIDER THIS:

Do you see pursuing justice, compassion, and service as distractions from the gospel?

On the other side, some pointed out that slavery was still thriving, though in the shadows. The May 16 editorial page cited how Chinese girls were being trafficked to Omaha, Nebraska for prostitution. On May 30 M. A. Cox pointed out that slavery was still thriving globally and since the Free Methodist Church was founded as a global movement, missionaries and those based outside of the United States were counting on the church to hold firm and keep the language in the Book of Discipline. F. D. Brooke appropriately affirmed this, commenting on Sept. 5 that while slavery has been legally abolished its spirit still lives, therefore Free Methodists should keep the language.

Mixed in with the conversation about slavery was a discussion of whether or not, and how, the races should "co-mingle." Some Free Methodists, while they believed the institution of slavery was evil and should be abolished, were nevertheless racists. They wanted to keep whites and "colored people" separate.

The following quote from a "colored" woman, Melinda Suggs, in July 11, 1899 is deeply moving. On the one hand it shows the openness of the Free Methodist system to hear from all, regardless of gender and/or color. There is tension in the system, but that's not a bad thing. We are truly "working out our salvation with fear and trembling."[3]

On the other hand, it also clearly shows the deep divide between black and white at the turn of the 20th Century. Declaring a people free does not make them so. Here is a great example of emancipation versus liberation. The Emancipation Proclamation set people free, but it was - and still is - up to all of us to make the words of the document truly live in our values, words, and actions. The divide is still there. We have more work to do.

> *I was born in slavery in Alabama. I have felt and seen what neither pen nor tongue can tell of its terrible oppressiveness. I saw my own mother beaten until her back was a mass of wounds and blood, and sent with no healing medicine–not even washed–into the field to fill her place with the rest. For days, feverish and sick as she was, she suffered and labored until it made me heartsick. A kick in the eye at the same time caused a breaking of the tear gland, which never was healed. Her crime was that she fell asleep about midnight as she sat by the fire watching her master's supper to keep it warm for him while he was away on a drunken spree. Coming home drunk and finding his supper grown cold, he beat her as I have described. This is only a faintly-drawn picture; one of many which are stamped on the memory of my childhood in slavery.*
>
> *Brother Kelly [a previous letter in The Free Methodist] suggested the idea of my colored brethren desiring to worship in separate congregations. Brethren, if they do, it is because they are made to feel that they are not wanted with the white brethren, or else they need the blood that sanctifies to take partiality and the fear of man out of their hearts. Since God has sanctified me I have had no respect of persons. I believe God "has made of one blood all nations" of the earth, as he has said; and because he has made one with white skin and straight hair and another with dark skin and curly hair does he love one more than another? If he does not, ought his children do so?*

> *If Jesus were on earth and should go into the Southern states to preach the gospel, do you think he would be pleased to have it as I have often seen it – the colored people allowed seats in the extreme back part of the church, if the congregation was small, and if it was large they must stand outside and look in at the windows?*
>
> *But my brother says "the rule is a dead letter [the statement in the Book of Discipline against slavery]." The letter may be dead, but can any impartial person suppose that the Spirit of slavery does not exist? The hatred and contempt, which to some extent are controlled by the law, are they not still there, burning with increased vehemence. . . ? And is not the living issues of the Free Methodist church, backed by the Holy Ghost power, coming in contact with this old spirit that makes the stir? I say brethren, Let it stir. Let the South, North and every part of the land know that the Free Methodist church will not take one step toward a compromise with any spirit but that which makes us all one in Christ Jesus our Lord. It may have to go slow in the South, but God will see it through.*
>
> *Is it not avoiding the real issue, to represent the action of striking out the clause as simply getting rid of an encumbrance? Will not such a representation mislead many of my good brethren who do not see the importance of this matter?*[4]

The statement remained in the Book of Discipline until 1974, when it was finally removed.

CONSIDER THIS:

Do you see racism in your church community? How does your church dialogue about this?

In 2007 issues of slavery again confronted the Free Methodist Church. At the General Conference that year the denomination voted unanimously to work to end modern slavery in all its forms with whatever means the Holy Spirit would direct. Another decisive step was taken in 2015, including a statement in the 37th Book of Discipline, which expressed the Free Methodist Church's convictions and commitments to engage in hopeful solutions to address slavery. It outlines how we must seek holistic freedom in all aspects of the church in ways that will spill out into the community. All of this is to do be done within a spirit of Jesus-centered community, collaboration, discipleship, and worship.[5] (See Appendix A at the end of the book for the full statement.)

Free Methodists are called "free" for a reason.

CONSIDER THIS:

Do you see the role of worship as a catalyst for action?

WORKING AGAINST RESISTANCE

All organizations have to watch out for mission drift. The mission and vision are initially clear, but over time, with multiple distractions, challenges, and opportunities, organizations get a little or a lot off track. Leaders know this. There is no such thing as balance, but rather balancing. Leadership teams ask hard questions and work to reduce the swing of focus, trying to keep the mission and vision clear. This is no less true for the church.

There are some people within the Free Methodist Church today who would steer the denomination toward a bland evangelicalism, seeing justice issues in the same way some did in 1899: as an obstacle to the gospel. Certain churches argue that the "real work" of the church is evangelism and church planting, and justice distracts us from those things. But given our history, our values, and the mission of Jesus, it's incomprehensible to have Free Methodist leaders challenging the work of justice within the Free Methodist Church.

As we've discussed, our journey is toward shalom. Set Free Movement leaders aren't just working toward freeing people from physical slavery, but are seeking freedom in every possible way by building communities where people can heal emotionally from hurt, leaders can develop, and people can come to know, love, and worship Jesus. We do this through strong partnership with church planters, national leaders, missionaries, and other organizations and denominations.

We're guided by three important points. First, if you've read all that has been written so far, we don't need to continue pointing out that our God is a God of justice, mercy, and compassion and that we are called to be on mission with God by bringing hope and healing to our broken world. There is no room-none-for blandness. Being on mission with God is thrilling. If you are part of a church teaching that justice is a distraction from the real work of the church, challenge the leadership. Don't run. With grace and humility, use scripture and history to point out how this thinking opposes Christian values.

Second, as an extension of the first point, we are a people that center on Jesus and pursue justice. Our history shows this over and over again. We must consider how justice integrates into the work of the church:

> *Church planting toward what?*
> *Evangelism to what end?*
> *Leadership development and partnering strong for what reasons?*
> *Why make disciples?*

The answers should be: to focus people on the person and work of Christ, to foster character and values that lead to holiness, and to continue to partner with the mission of God. Justice is part of this. A big part. We cannot plant churches that aren't founded on the principles of justice that Jesus established. We can't evangelize without addressing people's physical, mental, emotional, or relational needs. We cannot develop leaders or cultivate disciples who ignore justice.

Like the pastors in India who participate in brothel raids, we believe church leaders are well-poised to guide their congregations towards seeking freedom for others. In the Philippines, our Set Free Movement team has focused on providing specialized anti-trafficking training for pastors. Over the course of several days, the pastors are immersed in Philippine child protection and anti-trafficking laws. They learn how to report child abuse, domestic violence, and labor exploitation, as well as identifying the vulnerabilities that may lead up to these abuses in the first place. The vision is that these pastors will have the capacity to prevent and intervene in abuse within their church and community, and to mobilize their church to be part of the solution. Pastors might go on to lead conversations about families becoming foster care parents especially for children who have been abused or trafficked. They might fundraise for local child protection initiatives or encourage young people to consider studying to become professionals in social work, counseling, or related fields. They will disciple the members of their church to evangelize and seek justice as indivisible parts of the same goal.

Third, we believe that justice makes Jesus tangible.

I was at a Passion conference a few years ago at the Georgia dome, just down the street from CNN. Jesus was the center of the conference. The worship was incredible. Justice for those trapped in slavery was a strong focus.

CNN took notice, but they didn't care much about Jesus or the music. Instead they wanted to know why 60,000 young people were interested in ending modern slavery. Later, when hearing Louie Giglio, the founder and driver of Passion, debrief about the event he pointed out something powerful: when we engage in justice Jesus becomes tangible. When we do things like visiting the sick, feeding the hungry, freeing slaves, and comforting the wounded, we are the very presence of Jesus in the midst of the need. No longer is Jesus just a story in a book, a theological problem to solve, a reason for a holiday. No. When we care for others Jesus becomes tangible in our words and deeds.

Living out Jesus' call of justice and freedom is one of our greatest witnesses.

QUESTIONS FOR FURTHER REFLECTION:

Did you know about the history of the Free Methodist Church? What are your thoughts knowing in brief the things mentioned in this chapter?

About the statement from the Book of Discipline: how is your church working to fulfill these ideas?

What do you think about the strong statements regarding the role of justice in the church?

Do you think of service/justice as a distraction or as a secondary pursuit? Why? Why not?

How are you serving in your community? How is Jesus being made tangible in your actions?

ANNOTATIONS

1) "The Trip to the West," *EC* 4, no. 1 (July 1862): 30.

2) Howard A. Snyder, *B.T. and Ellen Roberts and the First Free Methodists*. Abridged Edition of *Populist Saints: B.T. and Ellen Roberts and the Early Free Methodists*, by Daniel V. Runyon. (Indianapolis: Committee on Free Methodist History and Archives Marston Memorial Historical Center, 2011), 486.

3) Philippines 2:12.

4) Melinda Suggs, "A Colored Woman on the Anti-slavery Rule," Chicago: *The Free Methodist*, (July 11, 1899), 5.

5) *Book of Discipline*, Indianapolis: Free Methodist Publishing House, 2016, 48-49.

See Appendix B to rank the way your church or group represents the values of discipleship and justice.

CHAPTER 8

ABANDONING COMMUNITY

> "For where two or three gather in my name, there am I with them."
> **Matthew 18:20**

In the small and unassuming Belgian town of Geel, a unique and perhaps unusual tradition has prevailed since the 15th Century. As they have since 1480, members of the town welcome people—strangers—with mental illness into their homes as an alternative to institutionalization. It's a sort of foster care system for the mentally ill but without age restrictions.

After psychiatric treatment and assessment, the participant is placed in a home in Geel and is now welcomed as a guest or boarder, not as a patient. The boarder is cared for—sometimes for years—by a family that receives a minimal stipend from the government. Hospitalization for the boarder is still an option if needed, and the host family does receive training and support from psychiatric professionals. However, the heart of the program is relationships, tolerance, and compassion, with some level of management and systems to help guide it.

With centuries of this practice being the norm, and with as much as a quarter of the town's population being boarders, the idea of mental illness has normalized and little distinction is drawn between the well and unwell. The boarders live with dignity, not viewed as an anomaly, burden, or source of fear.

Experimentation in providing humane care for people with mental illness has happened all around the world, but perhaps the secret to Geel's success is that the people in the town see community-based housing as normative. Nobody receives trophies or special status for being a host family. It's simply a part of the lifestyle and time-honored identity of the members of Geel.

REBUILDING SOCIAL STRUCTURES

In 2000 Robert Putnam published Bowling Alone, a book calling attention to the alarming collapse of social capital in the last half of the 20th Century. According to Putnam, one-third of America's civic infrastructure evaporated in the last three decades of the 20th Century.[1] Pressures on time and money, suburbanization, electronic entertainment, and generational change contributed to the breakdown of relational community structures.[2] Place-based social capital has been replaced by function-based social capital.[3] In other words, special interest groups with a programming and project mentality are competing with genuine community. Hence the title of his book–there used to be bowling leagues, but now we are bowling alone.

CONSIDER THIS:

Do you participate in organized sports?

Putnam points out that this is problematic. Civic infrastructure is built upon mutual reciprocity and trustworthiness, which are community assets.[4] Social capital allows citizens to resolve collective problems more effortlessly. It greases the wheels, allowing communities to advance smoothly while widening awareness of how all people in community are connected for the mutual good of all.[5] High levels of social capital, all else being equal, translate into lower levels of crime.[6] Social capital improves people's lives: even health is affected by social capital, since wellbeing is tied to healthy community.[7]

Child development is also powerfully shaped by social capital.[8] According to John McKnight and Peter Block, there is no "youth problem." There is, instead, a neighborhood problem.[9] Social capital and thick social connections form a safe, caring place where children and youth can thrive.[10] Cultures of compassion and support, both personal and local, are needed for the good of all.[11]

CONSIDER THIS:

How do your relationships with others help you to live well?

What led to the collapse of social capital? McKnight and Block point out two key reasons. First, management and institutions are given too great a priority over community. These structures seek predictability, order, and control, working to eliminate surprise.[12] By their nature and operation management and instructions cannot provide satisfaction and care because they seek to eliminate what is personal and human.[13] Like the community members of Geel, care is what neighbors do for each other. Care cannot be programmed or purchased.[14]

CONSIDER THIS:

How do you care for your neighbors?

Second, our way of thriving as satisfied citizens living in community has been replaced by being consumers in a managed, systematized world. Citizens and consumers are two different things. A citizen participates in democracy, using their gifts relationally to build up the community.[15] A consumer surrenders to management and institutions and purchases to fill the void.[16] Being a consumer breeds individualism, entitlement, and self-interest–the very things that work against community.[17] Such insatiable desires as these set the consumer up for a life that can never satisfy. It creates "an incomplete life. A life where the harder we try, the more hollow it becomes. Individuals become useless, families lose their function, neighborhoods lose their competence. We are then left to purchase what we might have chosen to produce."[18]

Instead of abandoning community and choosing to be controlled as consumers, we must advocate a return to community. McKnight and Block suggest that citizens unite to create abundant communities built on three properties: (1) gifts of the members; (2) rich associational life; and (3) hospitality, the welcoming of strangers. In turn these three properties foster the capacities of kindness, generosity, cooperation, forgiveness, acceptance of fallibility, and mystery.[19]

CONSIDER THIS:

How do you use your spiritual gifts to serve and bless others?

We do need some level of management, systems, programs, and control, but not at the expense of community. In abundant, competent communities, citizens organize around gifts, relationships, and hospitality and control is replaced by requests.[20] Focusing on problems is replaced by focusing on gifts and assets.[21] Self-interest is replaced by hospitality.[22] Quality of relationships, not wealth, position, or power, becomes the true measure of success.[23]

EMPHASIZING RELATIONSHIPS

One of the problems with programming justice is that it can sometimes do the exact opposite of its intention to build dignity. Programs, even unintentionally, turn people into "target groups" or "beneficiaries" which can be dehumanizing and creates an imbalance of power. Without even knowing it, we sometimes perform a triage to divide people into different levels of vulnerability and assign them terms such as "needy"–as if we don't all experience seasons of neediness or brokenness or vulnerability. This sets us up for a paternalistic relationship. We assume what people's needs are and build programs around them, and then congratulate ourselves for meeting our own targets.

This was the case in the remote Cambodian village of Sre Veng,[24] where clean water is a scarce resource. Dozens of people in this small community die each year from the harmful microorganisms and pollutants from water gathered from the nearby stream. An American non-governmental organization heard about this issue and decided to help the people of Sre Veng. They sent a team to the village to introduce bio-sand filters, an effective but simple new water filtration system. It was a system that had been widely successful in parts of West Africa, so surely it would help mitigate problems here. After the NGO staff constructed a filter for each family, they promised to return after awhile to see how they were doing.

About six months later, two NGO staff returned to Sre Veng to check in. They stopped at the first water filter they saw outside one family's house and lifted the lid. Both were shocked when, instead of seeing murky water being filtered through layers of gravel, they saw a heap of discarded soda cans, plastic bags, and other debris. The family was using the bio-sand filter as a garbage can.

Instead of engaging in prayer and assessing the village's needs in consultation with the people living in it, this NGO behaved as "saviors" and leapt straight into action. They made conclusions about the needs of others without asking them about it first.

It doesn't have to be this way. Ministries such as Refuge in Wichita know how to put community and human dignity ahead of systems. People who use the food pantry can choose their own basic needs items, which gives them a greater sense of responsibility and dignity than being handed a sack with pre-selected items. For the community members in Geel, there is indeed a place for screenings and organization, but not as the focus. The focus is on relationships that welcome and empower people with mental illness instead of making them feel like passive recipients of aid.

CONSIDER THIS:
Are you a citizen or a consumer?

Rather than focusing on problems, deficiencies, programs, entitlement, and interests, we should emphasize relationships and possibilities. Problem solving focuses on the wrong thing. Concentrating on what's wrong is simply looking at the symptoms of what are much deeper issues. Instead of looking at the problems of the community, we should focus on the breakdown of the community, addressing its health and functionality.[25]

CONSIDER THIS:
Do you focus on problems or possibilities?

What's interesting to me about the expertise from the authors above is that none of them are people of faith. They are clearly describing what I've been advocating for based on scripture and history. However, as I travel and speak about engaging in justice and working to end modern slavery from a community-based approach, some in the church don't get it. They want a program. They want curriculum. Some church leaders don't seem to understand what community is, why it's important, and how to create it. This is deeply troubling. But it doesn't mean we can't get back on track.

As we discussed in chapter 7, mission drift is common within churches. What we need are people—someone like you—who can help bring your church back into focus. This takes time and patience. As said by Jim Rohn, "you cannot change your destination overnight, but you can change your direction overnight."

Especially for church ministries, missionaries, or non-profits seeking God's heart for transformation above the human desire to implement projects and fix problems, it's likely they will face the challenge of communicating and validating their approach. It's simple to showcase a ministry's progress when there are tangible checklist items that can be ticked off: X blankets distributed, Y people fed, Z children rescued. It becomes much more difficult to measure hearts changed, values shifted, and communities drawn closer.

We have run into these same challenges at the Set Free Movement. We understand the necessity of having evaluation tools, organizational systems, and goals. But we also do our best to keep the focus of shalom in all we do, from meetings to administrative tasks to frontlines work.

QUESTIONS FOR FURTHER REFLECTION:

How have you experienced loss of community? How do you work to build social capital?

How do you resist becoming a consumer? How do you pursue being a fully engaged citizen?

Henri Nouwen defines "hospitality" as "making room for others." How do you make room for others? How do you practice your hospitality?

How does your church work to build community? What are some of the constraints keeping you or your church / group from focusing on relationships? How can you mitigate those constraints?

Do you know your gifts? How do you use them and build others up to use them? If you're working through this book as a group, list the gifts of the others in your group and share them.

ANNOTATIONS

1) Robert Putnam, *Bowling Alone* (New York: Simon and Schuster, 2000), 43.

2) Ibid., 283-284.

3) Ibid., 184.

4) Ibid., 134-136.

5) Ibid., 288-299.

6) Ibid.,308.

7) Ibid., 326.

8) Ibid., 296.

9) McKnight and Block, *Locations* 183-185.

10) Ibid., *Locations* 447-448.

11) Ibid., *Location* 820.

12) Ibid., *Locations* 576-586.

13) Ibid., *Locations* 595-598.

14) Ibid., *Locations* 186-188.

15) Ibid., *Locations* 215-216.

16) Ibid., *Locations* 229-230.

17) Ibid., *Locations* 1141-1150.

18) Ibid., *Locations* 1102-1104.

19) Ibid., *Locations* 1180-1184.

20) Ibid., *Locations* 1402-1403.

21) Peter Block, *Community: The Structure of Belonging* (San Francisco: Berrett- Koehler, 2008), 14.

22) McKnight and Block, *Locations* 1365-1369.

23) Ibid., 5.

24) Name of village has been changed.

25) Ibid., 32-40.

SECTION 3

WHERE DO WE GO FROM HERE?

CHAPTER 9

WE ARE NOT POWERLESS

> Now to him who is able to do immeasurably more than all we ask or imagine, according to his power that is at work within us.
> **Ephesians 3:20**

In their journey to open Eden's Glory, a restoration home for survivors of human trafficking, Ginger and Annie knew they would face tremendous challenges, setbacks, and spiritual warfare along the way. As the two leaders at the helm of the planning, Ginger and Annie knew even with the most dedicated and passionate team to support the work, there would be little fruitfulness without Jesus as their foundation.

Prayer guided everything they did. Prayer was what brought their group together in the first place. Prayer was the backbone of every meeting, every decision, every step. Before the walls of Eden's Glory were painted, members of the community wrote prayers in ink on every wall to literally surround the women with truth, scripture, and prayer. Their ask was simple but profound: for God to do immeasurably more than they could imagine.

And God did. The house itself had been gifted to the team, along with its five acres of land. While funds for renovating the house were coming out of the pockets of team members, local businesses and families provided financing, materials, and installation. Supplies didn't run out, even when they should have. Miracles were already starting to happen even before Eden's Glory opened.

Once the first few women moved into Eden's Glory, prayer requests would often be sent out to members of the community through text messages. When the residents battled spiritual warfare, community members would come to the chapel next door to Eden's Glory to pray over the women. There has been no shortage of struggle, but with their action being formed by prayer, their work being done in community, and their hearts pursuing the glory of God, they are seeing transformation in small and mighty ways.

THE HOW AND THE WHY

The Holy Spirit is the architect of our community. Only when we are centered on the person and work of Jesus, through the Spirit's power, guidance, fruit, and gifting, that we can be the people of God on mission with God. It is the Spirit, poured out upon all believers, who pulls all believers together into community. Ephesians 3:14-21 is key for understanding this:

> For this reason I kneel before the Father, from whom every family in heaven and on earth derives its name. I pray that out of his glorious riches he may strengthen you with power through his Spirit in your inner being, so that Christ may dwell in your hearts through faith. And I pray that you, being rooted and established in love, may have power, together with all the Lord's holy people, to grasp how wide and long and high and deep is the love of Christ, and to know this love that surpasses knowledge–that you may be filled to the measure of all the fullness of God.
>
> Now to him who is able to do immeasurably more than all we ask or imagine, according to his power that is at work within us, to him be glory in the church and in Christ Jesus throughout all generations, for ever and ever! Amen.

The progression is important to note. Paul begins by pointing back to the beginning of time when God created every family. He prays for an outpouring of riches, a divine inheritance, to empower the people of God. This is accomplished through the Holy Spirit.

The goal of this outpouring is for faith, rooted in Jesus. This is the beginning place. When we think about how to address real problems, correct injustice, and end modern slavery our predominant focus cannot be on the action or the problems. For Christians our focus is on Jesus and the empowerment of the Holy Spirit. Faith is founded on Jesus. Christians gather in the name of Jesus. Jesus is the foundation, the source, and the reason for both the "being" and the "doing." Authority and power are inseparably linked to the name, the person, and the work of Jesus.

It's not just about the "what," but the "how" and the "why" also. What is done cannot be spoiled by poor methods, which defeat the goal sought. E. Stanley Jones, one of the great 20th century missionaries, drives this point home: "The crusaders conquered Jerusalem and found in the end the Christ was not there. They had lost him through the very spirit and methods by which they sought to serve him. Many more modern and more refined crusaders end in that same barrenness of victory.[1]

CONSIDER THIS:

Is everything you are and do centered on Jesus?

It's not only about action, but it's about community-based, spirit-filled, prayer-formed action centered on Jesus and pursued for the glory of God. In commenting on Ephesians 2:8-10, professor and theologian Howard Snyder reminds us that God's plan is accomplished through the redeemed community, the church, by what it is and by what it does, but the church is before it does.[2]

Doing naturally flows out of Being. Eden's Glory is an excellent example of this. Their team did exactly what Proverbs 4:23 and Matthew 5-7 illustrate: how works of justice, charity, and service flow out of the faith community. Opening the restoration home simply wouldn't have been possible without prayer and the compassion of Christians in their community who were on mission with God.

The church is alive to God and lives to fulfill the will of God. What is the will of God? It is to establish the Kingdom of God in shalom, to bring humanity back to the beginning, righting the wrongs in a new creation, through Jesus.

Often we get stuck in black-or-white thinking. We see things as right or wrong. It's helpful to think more in terms of a continuum from incomplete to complete. It's true that evangelism is about converting people to truth, but that's incomplete. Kingdom life and salvation in Jesus are not just about converting individuals to truth. Individuals and society need to be recreated, transformed, and returned to lives of faith. Transformation of the individual and the society, from the inside out, from the heart flowing out into the community, is the goal. Shalom is the goal. Justice is a key to this and is the DNA of the church.

CONSIDER THIS:

Is evangelism primarily about converting people to truth or the first step in the discipleship process?

In Paul's prayer, faith in Jesus and the empowerment of the Spirit leads to love and more power and a deeper understanding of the love of Jesus. This love is beyond all knowledge. Fullness of faith, love, and power, centered on Jesus, is what we seek.

In Ephesians 3:20 Paul then shifts the prayer and reminds the faithful that God can do more than is asked or imagined. And the work of God, the more that is asked or imagined, flows out of the community of the saints with, for the third time in this prayer, power! In verse 21 God's glory is evident in the church and in Jesus. This is a powerful statement. The church is God's glory, filled up, empowered, together with Jesus. Note that Paul ends his prayer back at the beginning, focusing on the family.

CONSIDER THIS:

How do you use the power of God to live and help others around you?

The passages before and after this one focus on the community of the saints: Gentiles and Jews are together the church (3:6). This church is called, gifted, and on mission with God, equipped for service. It is the Spirit that unifies (4:3, 4). The Spirit fills (5:18) and leads the faithful in worship (5:19). The Spirit helps the Christian pray (6: 18) and is a penetrating sword (6:17).

The Spirit's filling in Ephesians 5:18 is in the Greek imperative and the following admonitions (1) speaking, (2) singing, (3) making music, (4) giving thanks, (5) submitting, all are dependent on the filling of the Spirit. The Spirit is the one that makes all these actions possible–and not just these–but all actions of the believer are dependent upon the Spirit. This leads to a crucial next point.

Instead of treating symptoms as if they are problems, the focus should shift to the possibility of community. Instead of honing in only on individual responses, there should be a collective engagement. Instead of solving problems we should be seeking transformation. Christian community is the social context for the supernatural transforming work of the Holy Spirit. And transformation is the work of a community.

When the shift moves from problems to possibilities and from individual solutions to community-based action, hope, then, becomes realized. We transition from seeing modern slavery as another problem to solve to recognizing it as a symptom of a bigger problem: brokenness. God, through Jesus, has already solved this bigger problem, and is even now healing us. This does not minimize the seriousness of the issue. Rather, this reframing shifts the focus to a hopeful alternative.

The primary work of the church is to seek the "shalom of the city" or, more precisely, the shalom of all that is broken, warped, and distorted. This includes proclaiming a new vision of unity, healing, and hope under the Lordship of Jesus.

Robert Linthicum, urban pastor and community organizer, wrote one of the most important books about engaging within an urban context, Transforming Power: Biblical Strategies for Making a Difference in Your Community. He writes:

> The work of the church goes far beyond preaching the gospel, winning souls to Christ, building up or planting congregations, working for social justice, or even hunkering down in order to preserve the church and to stay alive ... the work of the church is to hold up ... an entirely different vision for their society–a vision for all of life lived in shalom under the authority of Christ and manifested in that society's pursuit of a politics of justice, an economics of equitable distribution of wealth, the elimination of poverty and a people in relationship with God. And that "mystery" can only be realized if the church will move beyond itself to be engaged in every possible way in public life.[3]

It's not only about what we need to do as a church, but how we engage. Relationships within the trinity are based on love; therefore, love should define how the church operates. This love is seen powerfully in the incarnational approach to transformation whereby the follower of Christ, through authentic humility, lays aside agendas and power and seeks the greater good by becoming "one of us."

The people of God, the church, are more than a once-a-week gathering of likeminded people struggling through life. The people of God are a powerful force for good in the world, centered on Jesus and empowered by the Holy Spirit. With Jesus as its bedrock, the church is not powerless in the face of great problems.

After many years of prayer and a few years of being officially opened, is Eden's Glory still seeing God's power at work through the staff and volunteers? The answer is an undeniable yes. True transformation and healing is happening. Some of the residents are experiencing the longest stretch of sobriety since childhood. One woman is pursuing her GED, which is also a spiritual victory since she'd always believed the enemy's lie that she would never be smart enough to complete school. Another received several visions of her life being restored by Jesus and ended up giving her heart to him.

Not only are their lives being filled with love, support, and healing, but several of them are starting to give back, too. One of the ladies is working with at-risk youth. Others are volunteering at local nursing homes and singing in church choirs. They've initiated a fundraiser for a homeless family in their community.

This is God doing immeasurably more than could be asked or imagined. This is God's power working through humble, faithful servants who are redeeming lives. This is the church at its best.[4]

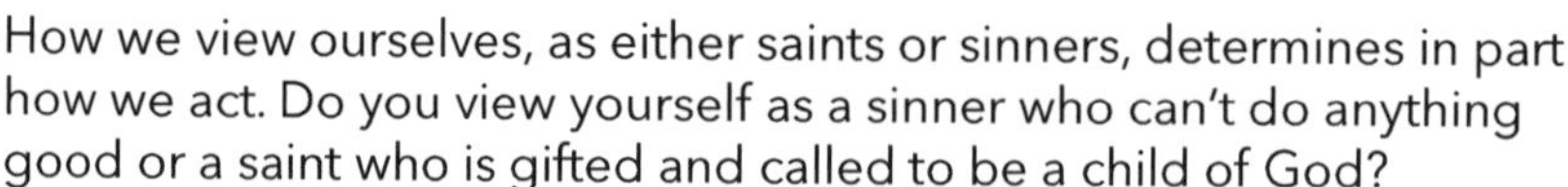

QUESTIONS FOR FURTHER REFLECTION:

How we view ourselves, as either saints or sinners, determines in part how we act. Do you view yourself as a sinner who can't do anything good or a saint who is gifted and called to be a child of God?

How are you working to be rooted and established in love with all the other saints around you?

Ephesians 1:19-20 states that we live in the power of the resurrection. Is this encouraging to you? In what ways?

One thing we in the Set Free Movement suggest people do is at 3:20 in the afternoon pray Ephesians 3:20 about whatever is happening at the time. Will you join us?

How does your church "hold up an entirely different vision" to your city?

ANNOTATIONS

1) E. Stanley Jones, *Christ at the Round Table* (New York: The Abingdon Press, 1928), 11.

2) Howard Snyder. *The Community of the King*. Downers Grove: Intervarsity Press, 2nd edition, 2004, 85.

3) Robert Linthicum, *Transforming Power: Biblical Strategies for Making a Difference in Your Community*. Downers Grove: Intervarsity, 2003, 127.

4) Find out more at www.edensglory.org.

CHAPTER 10

WHATEVER YOU DO, DO IT IN THE DIRECTION OF FREEDOM.

> "May you be strengthened with all power, according to his glorious might, for all endurance and patience with joy, giving thanks to the Father, who has qualified you to share in the inheritance of the saints in light. He has delivered us from the domain of darkness and transferred us to the kingdom of his beloved Son."
> **Colossians 1:11-13**

I was speaking to a room full of youth at Spring Arbor Free Methodist Church, teaching them about human trafficking and modern slavery. At one point someone asked me: "What should we do about it?" My answer back was: "What do you already do? God has gifted you. Use who you are and what you do in the direction of freedom."

After thinking for a few minutes one of them said: "We like to jump, run, kick, and hit things!" I suddenly realized I was speaking to a group of athletes. They were all lean and into sports. I suggested they do exactly that in the direction of freedom. Afterwards I heard that they organized a 5K human trafficking awareness walk and run. They raised more than $6,000 for anti-trafficking efforts by running and walking in the direction of freedom.

We often don't make these kinds of connections between our existing skills and the role we could play. Many of us minimize our abilities and underestimate the power of our collective efforts. And that's understandable, knowing how overwhelming the issues around us are.

The abuse and harassment of women is one of those issues. CNN, and others, cite that 1/3 of women in our society have been sexually abused.[1] In the United States, an estimated 83 percent of girls ages 12 to 16 have experienced some form of sexual harassment in public schools.[2] Out of the women who are currently involved in prostitution, 95 percent were abused as children.[3]

Sexual abuse is not an isolated issue. In many cases, it can lead to sexual exploitation. Abuse can, therefore, be a stepping stone into modern-day slavery. Poverty is another stepping stone. So is environmental degradation.[4] So is coming from a family with addiction, violence, and neglect.

The problems to address are complex and endless. Finding individual solutions for the millions of orphans and slaves in our world is not possible. Innovative business ideas alone don't provide solutions. Better laws will help, but aren't the only answer. Academia is important for research and educating new leaders, but schools cannot change the world on their own.

If we want to end slavery or domestic violence or sexual abuse, we need to develop holistic, integrated solutions. We need to challenge and change the culture and the values of society that justify exploitation. As professor and theologian James Davison Hunter phrases it, "How do we redeem a culture? ... from the inside out. From the individual to the family to the community, and then outward in ever widening ripples."[5]

How does deep transformation of our society happen? By mobilizing every branch of society.

Abolitionists in 19th Century Britain are a model for us today. Deeply disturbed by slavery, the Quakers prayed for discernment in how to respond. God answered and the Quakers were compelled to quit eating sugar, which was planted, harvested, and shipped by slaves. Their boycott created economic pressure to change the way sugar was sourced.

But they weren't the only ones who responded. The power was in the way numerous sectors were mobilized to oppose slavery. Artists drew pictures to awaken people to the wrongness of slavery. Musicians wrote songs like "O Holy Night," an abolitionist agitator song–think of the line "chains he shall break for the slave is our brother"–which was outlawed when first written. Champions in parliament like William Wilberforce worked to craft laws that would abolish slavery.

In one generation slavery went from being fully accepted to completely rejected to the extent that British marines chased down ships carrying slaves. Every branch of society was involved. We can repeat this.

YOU HAVE A PLACE HERE

Rather than social change being programmed, controlled, and initiated by a few leaders, Set Free Movement leaders take a different approach. They advocate for an incarnational, discipleship driven, community framework, which includes grassroots activism that incorporates all the influencers of society. Faithful presence, smart action, and deep thinking discipleship result in cultural change.

We have a phrase we often use in the Set Free Movement: whatever you do, do it in the direction of freedom. To be part of this movement, you don't need to be anyone different–you simply need to be who God created you to be. Just like the young athletes at Spring Arbor Free Methodist Church, God has also given you gifts and talents that you can use in the direction of freedom.

Many of our Set Free Movement leaders have found clarity in their purpose within the modern-day abolitionist movement simply by fusing their skills and passions with God's call to seek justice for the oppressed. Sarah, one of our leaders in Tampa, Florida, is a nurse–she trains hospital staff on how to identify and appropriately help clients who may be victims of human trafficking. Cindy is a teacher and a traveler, so as she educates her community in Decatur, IL, and when she heads south in the winter, she hosts trainings in the campgrounds where she stays. George is a musician–so he pulled together a worship band called Set Free and uses concerts and dance performances to tell the story of modern slavery. Katie is a writer–she composes blog posts and magazine articles discussing current issues of human trafficking around the world.

We need songwriters, politicians, police, lawyers, business leaders, soccer moms, and prayer warriors. Everyone has a role to play. Curt, a friend of the Set Free Movement, is a great example of this. A keen business leader for nearly thirty years, Curt opened his first Subway Sandwich Shop in 1988 and doubled its sales within his first six months.

He began working as Development Agent for Subway and continued to open other restaurants, including the first Subway Shop in Prague, Czech Republic.

As his deep involvement in the restaurant industry continued to grow, so did his awareness that some store owners tended to employ people from certain ethnic groups almost exclusively. Finding this suspicious, he did some research and found out that these employees were indentured servants or slave laborers—something he had no idea was happening in his own country. He grew more invested in the issue, working with the authorities to intervene, but wanted to do even more.

When our paths crossed with Curt, our advice to him wasn't to quit his job, sell his businesses, and work full-time to combat slavery. Instead, we encouraged him to do what he does best: business. So, in the summer of 2016, Curt began using several of his Subway businesses as an outlet to educate his customers on the prevalence of human trafficking in their city in Michigan. He put up posters in his restaurant, trained his staff, engaged customers in conversations, and gave a portion of his profits to the Set Free Movement.

Today, we continue to rely on Curt for mentorship in strategic planning—a gap faced by many non-profits, who usually have good intentions and fervent passion but often lack business skills. Who he is and what he already does is one of the biggest ways he can contribute to the movement to end slavery. The same applies to you. How will you be part of the solution?

QUESTIONS FOR FURTHER REFLECTON:

What social issues are not being adequately addressed in your community?

Which sectors of society are the most and the least involved in justice issues within your community?

Quakers boycotted sugar, which was slave-made. What is one product or brand that uses slave labor that you could give up?

Take a moment to think about some of your own skills and passions. Where might there be a place for those things within this movement?

What are the strengths of your church or group? How can those strengths contribute to the work of justice?

ANNOTATIONS

1) Madison Park,"WHO: 1 in 3 women experience physical or sexual violence," *CNN*, June 20, 2013. http://www.cnn.com/2013/06/20/health/global-violence-women/.

2) Charles Blow, *Yes All Men*, June 1, 2014 New York Times http://nyti.ms/SnyqwQ.

3) Richard J. Estes and Neil Alan Weiner. *"The Commercial Sexual Exploitation of Children In the U. S., Canada and Mexico."* University of Pennsylvania, School of Social Work. Center for the Study of Youth Policy. September 18th, 2001.

4) Romina Picolotti, ed., and Jorge D. Taliant, ed., *Linking Human Rights and the Environment*, (Tucson: University of Arizona Press, 2003).

5) James Davison Hunter, *To Change the World: The Irony, Tragedy, and Possibility of Christianity in the Late Modern World* (New York: Oxford University Press, 2010), 8.

CHAPTER 11

SOCIAL ACTION AND DISCIPLESHIP

> Follow God's example, therefore, as dearly loved children and walk in the way of love, just as Christ loved us and gave himself up for us as a fragrant offering and sacrifice to God.
> **Ephesians 5:1-2**

You may recall we highlighted Eden's Glory in a previous chapter. This is how their story begins:

I had just finished spending several days speaking about freedom issues at Central Christian College in Kansas and the chaplain, Ginger Coakley, was driving me back to the airport. We had a life-changing conversation as we debriefed our time together and what might be next. She expressed that she was both compelled and convicted to help end modern slavery, but she wasn't sure what the next steps were. At that point it was early on in the history of the Set Free Movement, so I also was not entirely sure what it meant to meaningfully engage in the modern abolitionist movement.

When we think of "social action" we often think of a Greenpeace demonstrator in a rubber boat charging a whaling vessel, or people chanting and marching down streets with placards. And so, when people hear about human trafficking, they immediately think of rescuing women in chains from brothels. Certainly, there are times and places where these kinds of social actions are required, but the Set Free

Movement today takes a different approach.

Instead of social action, think discipleship.

Before leaping into action, the process by which the Set Free Movement does all of our work starts with a community of people gathering together for prayer and learning. Instead of being guided by the human ego of thinking we know what our community needs without consulting with it first, the Holy Spirit guides the work. We move into dialoguing and networking, then experimenting. Eventually–sometimes after several years (read that again: years, not days, weeks or months)–a team will be led by God to a strategy, which will be sustainable and transformative, built on the strengths and gifts of the team, informed by the needs and context of the community, and focuses on collaborating with others instead of recreating the wheel.

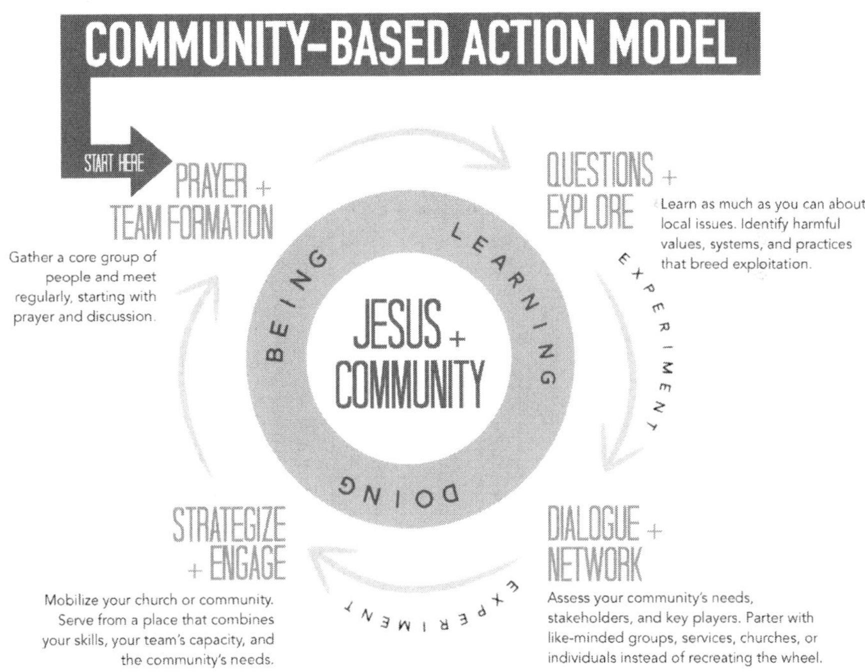

CONSIDER THIS:

Do you think about HOW you are acting in the same way that you think about WHAT you are doing?

We're led by this process because we've seen how frequently churches, non-profits, missionaries and activists emphasize WHAT they are doing and give little or no thought to HOW they are engaging. Too often we focus on the outcomes we want to see, giving little thought to the process. We say we believe in prayer and in the Holy Spirit, but we then work as if prayer is foolish and as if the Holy Spirit will not help. We need to repent of this.

We see how the Bible asks us to be aware of our motivations and strategies. I Corinthians 13 gives us a running list of good things to do, but if we don't have love, it's all in vain. 2 Timothy 2:5 even instructs us to be gentle with those who oppose us.

How we do things matters.

CONSIDER THIS:

How do you balance the "how" and "what" in your life?

DISCIPLESHIP

Discipleship is about character formation. It usually happens within a small community of people who come together to seek and learn about Jesus, worship and pray, and grow spiritually. Eventually, within this context of community, behavior changes and character is formed. The disciple becomes more and more like Christ. These changes are not just spiritual, but affect every area of life.

CONSIDER THIS:

What is your current experience with discipleship?

Discipleship is the engine of the church and of mission. It's more than just learning key concepts, having certain beliefs, and figuring out how to function within a body of believers. Discipleship is holistic, encompassing all of life. It's life-affirming, socially transformative, and existentially demanding.

Mission happens within the scope of discipleship. Perkins and Marsh write that "discipleship to Jesus Christ is the most enduring source of renewed social practices, care for the poor, costly forgiveness and reparations for slavery. Christian hope in our time demands that we reckon with this truth."[1] Similarly, Jim Martin, of International Justice Mission, explains how working to address violence, abuse, and oppression have presented ripe opportunities to share God. He suggests:

> What we've found is that the work of justice is some of the most fertile ground for discipleship that we've ever experienced. The places of violent oppression and abuse that may seem utterly God-forsaken are in fact the places where we have most deeply experienced the presence and power of God. The call to the work of justice is therefore not God sending his church out to a place where God cannot be found. Rather, God is inviting us into the place where he is already at work ... The call to fight against injustice is therefore the call to intimacy with God and to deep discipleship.[2]

The same applies to our approach at the Set Free Movement. Five main principles guide us. First, we believe the Holy Spirit directs our work. We know how easy it is to talk about the Holy Spirit, but often live as if the Holy Spirit isn't operating in, around, with, and through us. We pray for God to bless our plans then work as if God isn't helping us. This is backwards. Instead, we need to accept that "the church doesn't have a social strategy; the church is a social strategy."[3]

Second, Being precedes Doing. We are; then we do. God appeared to Moses and said, "I am." This statement of reality preceded the Exodus. Moses had a preparation time in the desert. God spoke to Moses, then acted. In the Set Free Movement, we engage in an important rhythm of prayer, lamenting, learning, simply being a presence in the midst of suffering without action. Later we strategize and act.

In discipleship character formation is everything. God creates us as new creatures with new values. As we live into being formed into the character of Christ our actions conform. The fruits of the Spirit flow out of character and worship, in harmony with the Holy Trinity.

Third, the process is just as important as the outcomes. This is a counter-cultural thought for most organizations–especially non-profits–where outcome is everything. But if we want to reduce vulnerabilities to human trafficking in a community, we must begin with who we are becoming in Christ. God initiates character formation. We must focus more on discipleship than projects and programs, asking ourselves these questions: What is our attitude when we serve? Are we approaching our work with love, humility, grace, and hope? Do we just go through the motions?

HOW is just as important as WHAT.

Fourth, all we are and do happens within the context of community. When the Set Free Movement hires an international leader, we don't start by creating job descriptions with lists to do. Instead, we begin by travelling to where they are and spend quality and quantity time with them. We get to know them, listen and laugh, and share life together. We emphasize community above all else. Together we work on vocational guidelines and then they, the international leader, creates the lists to do. Programs and projects are the end result of deep thinking, dialoguing, partnering, and prayer. Community comes first.

The Set Free Movement was birthed out of the Free Methodist Church USA, whose mission statement emphasizes that we are called to love both God and others, and also to make disciples. Christ didn't call us to plant churches, free slaves, or vote certain ways. Christ called us to make disciples. The movement of God, the mission of God, is organic. Discipleship is not optional. It's the power source of all we are and all we do.

SOCIAL ACTION

After that conference at Central Christian College in Kansas, Ginger was confronted with a million contrasting emotions. She couldn't believe that slavery has never been more rampant than it is today. It was hard enough for her to accept that a $150 billion criminal industry thrived off the slavery of millions of people around the world, but it devastated her when she discovered that human trafficking was occurring in her own quiet community in rural Illinois.

The question wasn't whether or not she was going to respond to the issue. The question was a matter of how. Every Monday morning at 7:00, she and her friend, Annie, would gather with one or two others at a coffee shop to pray that God would guide them through the murky waters of feeling overwhelmed and, at times, paralyzed. Months of steadfast prayer grew into research. Research grew into exploring different interventions, from awareness events to training frontlines workers.

The team began identifying gaps in their community and learned there were only eight beds available to offer recovery to survivors in Illinois. Ginger and her team knew what they needed to do: open a restoration home for women who have survived human trafficking, and to call it Eden's Glory.

But restoration homes don't spring up overnight. Ginger and Annie knew that if the home were to exist for the long-run, it needed to belong to the entire community. By investing the time into engaging all aspects of their community–businesses and faith leaders, schools and government–Ginger and Annie watched the community respond. The owner of a flooring business provided financing for beautiful laminate flooring and new carpets, which another family paid to have installed. Two local women dedicated their whole summer to painting walls, sewing curtains, and decorating the entire house. And now that the home is open, members of their community regularly devote their time, skills, and prayer to the women in residence.[4]

The pattern continues with the women they are serving. Giving these women a safe place to stay and nutritious food to eat is a small part of the mission. The goal is to see character being built and hearts being transformed. Discipleship is integrated into all aspects of the day for the women. After the women have spent two years in residence, the hope is that they will be fully confident in their relationship with Jesus and will go on to make disciples in others.

QUESTIONS FOR FURTHER REFLECTION:

Describe your current discipleship strategy.

If most injustices are symptoms, what are the underlying problems?

Evaluate briefly how you are feeling empowered by the Holy Spirit. What does it look like? How do you partner with the Holy Spirit?

How is your character currently being formed?

How do you evaluate your actions based on the above questions?

ANNOTATIONS

1) Wayne Gordon, John M. Perkins. *Making Neighborhoods Whole: A Handbook for Christian Community Development* (Downer's Grove: InterVarsity Press, 2013), Kindle Location 369-371.

2) Jim Martin, *The Just Church: Becoming a Risk-Taking, Justice-Seeking, Disciple-Making Congregation* (Chicago: Tyndale House, 2012), Locations 234-241.

3) William H Willimon and Stanley Hauerwas, *Resident Aliens: Life in the Christian Colony (Expanded 25th Anniversary Edition)* (Nashville: Abingdon Press, 2014) Kindle Electronic Edition, Locations 379-382; 634.

4) Find out more at www.edensglory.org.

CHAPTER 12

AGENTS OF HOPE AND HEALING

> Jesus went through all the towns and villages, teaching in their synagogues, proclaiming the good news of the kingdom and healing every disease and sickness.
> **Matthew 9:35**

> Therefore confess your sins to each other and pray for each other so that you may be healed. The prayer of a righteous person is powerful and effective.
> **James 5:16**

When Katie Bergman first stepped onto the mission field, her experience was not the mutual, relationship-driven model we've been discussing. And when it culminated in deep disillusionment and burnout, she knew something needed to change.

Ever since Katie was about seven years old, her heart was set ablaze to live out the call of Micah 6:8 to seek justice, love mercy, and walk humbly with God. After completing her degree in justice studies, Katie put her passion into practice and catapulted into international service by caring for orphans and at-risk youth, supporting people with mental illness and physical disabilities, helping to relieve poverty, and intervening in human trafficking.

But along the way, Katie was confronted by an unexpected paradox that was equally strange and profound. Although her purpose was to address brokenness in people and villages in other countries, she gradually started identifying hidden depths of brokenness within her non-profit—and in herself, too. She found it deeply unsettling to discover that the non-profit industry—which she'd always put up on a pedestal—was not the perfect place she'd imagined. She was confused by witnessing the corruption, spiritual manipulation, and ulterior motives of fellow Christian justice seekers. Slowly, she began asking herself if staying on the mission field would be worth it.

HEALING FOR THE HEALER

At this point a Wesleyan emphasis can be applied. Not only did Jesus die to save us from sin, but he also rose again to bring healing to a broken world. Jesus came to forgive sin, yes, but that foundational theology is incomplete. Jesus also heals our shame. Sin is doing wrong things, but shame is believing there is a deep flaw in who we are—in this sense we believe we are "a bad thing."

CONSIDER THIS:

Are you in need of healing? Do you see Jesus as the great physician?

In Wesleyan thought Jesus is, among other things, the great physician. Salvation includes healing from the damage of sin as well as release from the power of sin. The Holy Spirit is the agent who transforms fallen people into new creations, healed and empowered. Community and action are a means to the end that not only are wrongs righted, but people experience healing and hope—in other words, shalom flourishes.

Healing is linked to justice. Healing the marred identity of the poor is the beginning of transformation.[1] Transformation requires a disciplined and impassioned commitment to the healing of the social order.[2]

SMART ACTIVISM:
PARTNERSHIP-ORIENTED, COMMUNITY-BASED, HOLISTIC, GROUNDED IN SCRIPTURE

EDUCATION
PREVENTION
RESCUE
COLLABORATION AND PROGRAMS
RESTORATION
COMMUNITY MOBILIZATION

NEW FUTURES AND DEEP TRANSFORMATIONAL CHANGE

As we discussed in Chapter 8, programs alone don't create healing. Programs don't fix communities–neighbors do.[3] Healing begins and is sustained through human connection and community in partnership with God. These are the things that bring hope and healing to the world.

The need for hope and healing is reciprocal. It must belong to both the person caught in slavery or abuse and the person seeking to intervene. Many of our Set Free Movement leaders find that, as they work to reduce vulnerability, care for survivors, and end modern slavery, they discover their own chains and brokenness. Katie's story at the start of this chapter is one of many. Other members of our staff and volunteers come to the Set Free Movement with a long history of being convinced by our churches, workplaces, charities, or relationships that their value is in their productivity and performance. Pastors having more of a marriage to their church than their spouse. Burned out church members and volunteers turning their service into an idol that gives them a sense of worth or a distraction from family issues. Activists fighting against slavery by enslaving themselves to a cause.

The Set Free Movement seeks to break the cycle of abuse, sin, and shame that perpetuates modern slavery and other injustices. But that process applies to more than the people we help: the children being sexually exploited online in the Philippines, or the foster care children being trafficked across the U.S. We identify our own need for healing as we seek to bring healing in the lives of others.

The Set Free Movement is intentional about creating open and honest community where baggage can be laid out without shame, disillusionment can be spoken, and hurts can be shared. We strive to create a safe space where our leaders can pursue both freedom for others and for themselves as well. We seek to end modern slavery, but we identify our own need for liberation as we work to liberate others. We evaluate the success of our work based on the health of our teams and presence of community. Although we have our moments when we get more caught up in doing before being, we remember to re-center.

This brings us back to why the HOW is just as important as the WHAT. As servants of God and seekers of justice, we don't have it all figured it out. We are in need of rescue, hope, and healing also. Therefore, our work comes from a place of humility and is a continued process of identifying our mutual needs and limits.

Katie shares the rest of her story below, told from her own perspective.

A NEW KIND OF SERVICE

The further I went down the missional road, the more I started noticing how much skewed theology and hurting people comprised the non-profits for which I worked. Even in drastically different environments–from an evangelical mission in Mexico to a secular anti-trafficking start-up in cosmopolitan California, from an international development superpower in Cambodia to a small inner-city youth outreach center in Canada–a common philosophy prevailed: we are here to save but don't need saving. We are here to give but have no need to receive.

You could spot this paternalism everywhere, from our language to our programs to our prayers. We'd write up complex logical models and implement projects with little consultation of the people who would benefit from them. Several organizations I worked for had a presence on multiple continents but didn't know the name of any of the people we served—we simply referred to them distantly as "beneficiaries" or "stakeholders."

These dichotomies set us up for a transactional form of service, giving us quick and easy victories that made for persuasive donor letters and compelling websites. But our siloed and patronizing posture could only ever produce short-term, surface-level successes—not long-term, transformational change.

We were also trapped by the unconscious but dangerous belief that we were commissioned to be saviors. For myself, this was compounded by an entire lifetime of belonging to a faith that sometimes misinterpreted Christianity as perfection. I came to the mission field with an already convoluted standard of self-righteousness, which only escalated in an environment that reinforced martyrdom in all aspects of our work and spiritual lives. So, I carried the thorniest, most cumbersome cross I could find. It was a lonely path, but I dared not allow others to see me struggle for fear that it would compromise their perception of my commitment to the cause or my spiritual integrity.

Under the pressure to perform, my co-workers and I worked at such a vigorous pace it was as if we thought we could earn our salvation by it—a habit that even Christians outside of missions sometimes develop. We were walking ironies, enslaving ourselves to work that sought to end slavery and denying ourselves simple joys and even basic needs like sleep or lunch breaks to maximize our contributions to the work of alleviating poverty.

Chasing an unattainable standard bred the crippling shame of never being enough, which pushed me deeper into despair and further away from others. A few of the organizations I worked for capitalized on that, using my shame as a tool to keep me tied to the cause.

But after going too hard for too long, I went through a devastating burnout that brought me away from the field and into a painful spiritual battle and bout of depression that nearly put me in a hospital. I was unable to work, unable to think clearly, unable to enjoy any of my former hobbies and passions.

I was broken. Isolated. Without hope. Unable to meet my own needs.

There could be no more "us versus them" after an experience like that. I'd never been trafficked or involved in a gang or homeless, but now I knew what it was like to be broken, longing for healing; to be drained and dry, longing for restoration; to be lonely and lost, longing to be found. Now I could meet others in suffering not as an expert or even a Westerner, but as another human. I was released from the burden of saving and could simply be someone who helps and needs help in return. Finally, I had the freedom to be a human who makes mistakes and doesn't know all the answers, to ask for support and receive grace.

And in doing so, I could stop diametrically opposing joy and service, too. It had been difficult trying to be a beacon of light to a hurting community while I was living in darkness. I struggled to cultivate hope in others when I had none to begin with. But now, what building healthy communities means to me is investing in my own health; taking care of others requires me to take care of myself, too.

After a long break, I returned to the justice field with a renewed passion, stronger boundaries, and a different posture for serving: one of being in relationship with God and others. I'd realized that I hadn't been fully living out the call of Micah 6:8, the verse I'd proudly touted as my mantra, after all. I'd left out the latter part, walking humbly with God, because that means being, not doing. It means listening to God's heart for shalom above the noisy pressures of productivity and programming justice. It means accepting my limits, admitting my brokenness, and addressing my needs, which perhaps God gave me to turn me back to God in the first place.

Maybe we're all struggling with different things in the same world; all of us in need of love and grace, all of us wanting forgiveness and redemption, all of us having something we need and something we offer.

QUESTIONS FOR FURTHER REFLECTION:

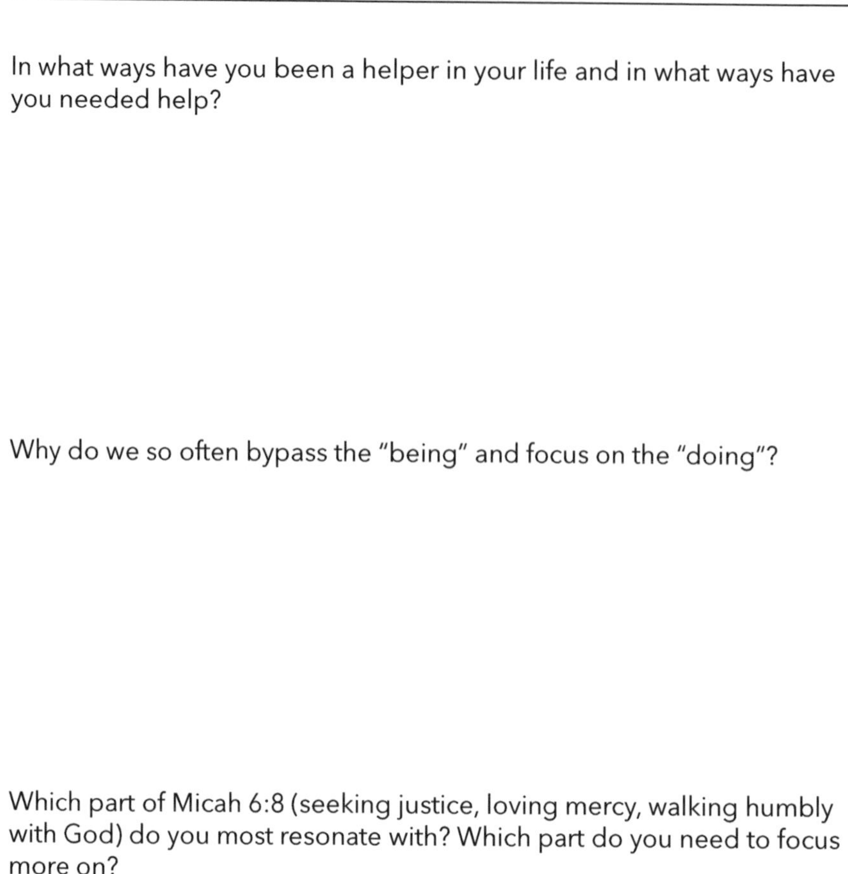

In what ways have you been a helper in your life and in what ways have you needed help?

Why do we so often bypass the "being" and focus on the "doing"?

Which part of Micah 6:8 (seeking justice, loving mercy, walking humbly with God) do you most resonate with? Which part do you need to focus more on?

In what ways have you separated joy or fun from serving or giving?

Does your church or group look at both the brokenness "out there" in the world as well as the brokenness within your community, church, or group?

ANNOTATIONS

1) Bryant L. Myers, *Walking With The Poor: Principles and Practices of Transformational Development* (Maryknoll: Orbis Books, 2011) Kindle Electronic Edition, Locations 3832.

2) John Perkins and Charles Marsh *Welcoming Justice: God's Movement Toward Beloved Community* (Downers Grove: InterVarsity Press, 2009) Kindle Electronic Edition, Location, 384.

3) Wayne Gordon, John M. Perkins. *Making Neighborhoods Whole: A Handbook for Christian Community Development* (Downer's Grove: InterVarsity Press, 2013), 50.

CHAPTER 13

LIVING INTO OUR HERITAGE

> Therefore, since we are surrounded by such a great cloud of witnesses, let us throw off everything that hinders and the sin that so easily entangles. And let us run with perseverance the race marked out for us, fixing our eyes on Jesus, the pioneer and perfecter of faith. For the joy set before him he endured the cross, scorning its shame, and sat down at the right hand of the throne of God. Consider him who endured such opposition from sinners, so that you will not grow weary and lose heart.
> **Hebrews 12:1-3**

B.T. Roberts, the founder of the Free Methodist Church, stood in the street and watched with wide eyes and growing righteous anger the sale of slaves in St. Louis. He saw the brokenness of the slaves and the casual opportunism of the buyers. He knew this was incompatible with the gospel of Jesus Christ and the mission of the church.

Although he would have righteous anger today at the slavery and brokenness he would see, B.T. Roberts would also be greatly encouraged to see the church globally working to end modern slavery holistically. He would especially have his heart warmed by how his denomination has stepped into the gap. But righteous anger and good feelings aren't the point.

Where do we go from here?

Until everyone is free there is work to do.

The scriptures convict and compel, informing and forming. Historical examples give testimony to the truth. Our society is in critical need. God is calling us to respond. Living out the mission statement of Jesus in Luke 4:19, this could be the favorable year of the Lord.

I now leave you with four invitations for moving forward.

CONSIDER THIS:

What would it look like for the "favorable year of the Lord" to come to your community?

---

1. ANSWER THE CALL

Whatever you do, whoever you are, you have a role to play. David Clemente, Justin Behrend, Wendy Shuffett, and Jeff McPherson are teachers who use their discipline in the direction of freedom. Halle Hemberry is a high school sophomore raising awareness in her school. George is a musician; Curt a businessman; Cindy is retired. You don't have to have it all figured out. You don't have to be any different than who you are–called, gifted, and chosen. Just be you in the direction of freedom.

2. PARTNER STRONG

Siddharth Kara, an expert on human trafficking, makes some important conclusions about why society to date has been ineffective in addressing modern slavery. According to Kara one of the things holding back progress is that "organizations are underfunded and uncoordinated."[1]

CONSIDER THIS:

How does your church partner with others in the community for the common good?

When, where, and how we can, we should seek to work together across denominational and organizational lines. The authors of the book Forces for Good examined thousands of non-profits and learned that there were six things than made a non-profit exceptional—and one of these was not being territorial and instead to partner strong.[2]

An example of this is how the Set Free Movement is partnering with the Salvation Army, the Church of the Nazarene, International Justice Mission, and World Hope International in Manila to address the problem of child trafficking, which is fueling cyber porn. The problem is too large for any one group to address. But it's not just about solving problems—it's about transforming society. We need everyone in order to do this, especially those who bring different skill sets and experiences than our own. Partnering strong with others is the second invitation.

CONSIDER THIS:

How do you live with this dual purpose, centering your life on Jesus while also living a holy life in thought, word, and deed?

---

3. DON'T SIMPLY EXIST, BUT LIVE FULLY

The genius of the original Wesleyan movement was the renewal of discipleship as the key for both holy living as well as church health and growth. As we've advocated in this book, a focus on discipleship as a means to informing social action is important. This is what the Set Free Movement seeks to do.

Here is the third invitation: you are invited to live into your heritage as a community of people who both love Jesus and pursue justice. We are on journey with the Israelites freed from slavery, with the disheartened on the road to Emmaus, and with the slave ripped from her homeland, thrown into the hold of the ship, and transported to a new land. We are part of a family who, though disillusioned and frustrated at times, has followed God into the unknown to make Jesus known. Our ancestors didn't go through the motions. They lived fully, vibrant lives. Let us do the same.

4. LEAN INTO HOPE

The last invitation is to live fully into the hope to which we have been called. There is a time to lament, but we must learn to grieve without despair. Yes, the problems are big. No, we don't have all the answers or always get it right. But Jesus was raised from the dead! Come on! There is nothing our God cannot do. Let us lean and live into hope and be a people of hope.

When you look at the Set Free Movement website you'll notice in whatever pictures you see that our team members are smiling, sometimes laughing, always balancing the seriousness of the calling with the celebration of life. There is no room for despair. We are on mission with God and it is a joyful experience.

QUESTIONS FOR FURTHER REFLECTION:

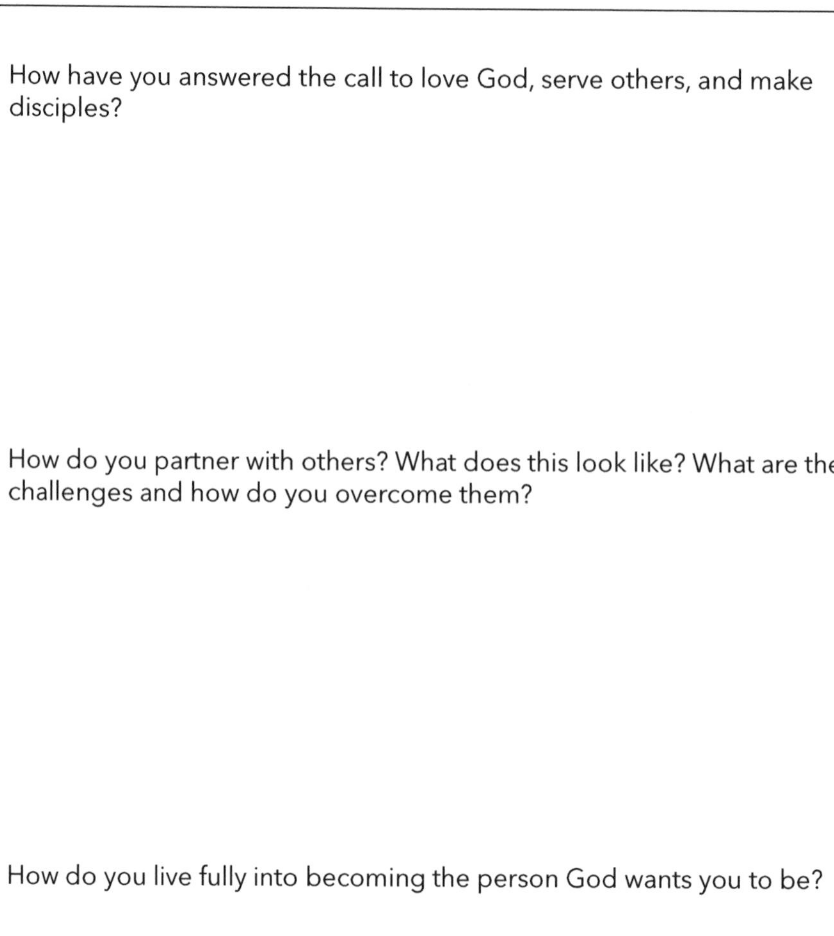

How have you answered the call to love God, serve others, and make disciples?

How do you partner with others? What does this look like? What are the challenges and how do you overcome them?

How do you live fully into becoming the person God wants you to be?

What gives you hope?

How do you cultivate hope?

ANNOTATIONS

1) Siddharth Kara, *Sex Trafficking Inside the Business of Modern Slavery* (New York: Columbia University Press, 2009), 3.

2) Leslie R. Crutchfield and Heather McLeod Grant, *Forces for Good: The Six Practices of High-Impact Nonprofits* (San Francisco: Jossey-Bass, 2008).

FURTHER STUDY

At this point, you might be wondering what's next for you, your group, or your church. We cannot answer that for you. We do not provide cookie-cutter strategies of engagement because every person and community is different. We do, however, have a few truthful statements we'd like to share with you. Read them out loud to yourself or to your group. Remind yourself of these things when you're overwhelmed or confused about which step to take:

- I am on mission with God.
- I will seek shalom, not only in my ministry but in my daily interactions with others.
- I will build community, seek partnerships, and tolerantly listen to perspectives different from my own.
- I will do my best to balance relationships, discipleship, justice, and compassion, knowing that each is equally important in building the Kingdom of God.
- I already have gifts, resources, compassion, knowledge, time, and a sphere of influence that I can use for good.
- I cannot be a savior or carry the burdens of the world but I can do small things that are powerful when done in community and sustained over time.
- I am not completely complacent in the world's brokenness. But I will not allow guilt to consume me, shame to paralyze me, or fear to keep me from seeking justice.
- I will examine how my own prejudices quietly fuel acts of exclusion or hatred.
- I will examine how my lifestyle choices, including my purchasing habits, tread on the freedom and dignity of others.
- I have done bad things but that does not make me a bad thing. I am one of God's chosen people and special possessions.
- I cannot undo evil that has been done to me or to others but I can deliberately focus on hope, joy, and the good–not to diminish injustice but to intentionally invest my energy in healthy ways.
- I will pray that God will do immeasurably more than I could ask or imagine.

APPENDIX A:

MODERN SLAVERY IN THE FREE METHODIST CHURCH BOOK OF DISCIPLINE

Issues surrounding modern slavery/human trafficking* in the United States and globally are complex. They require solutions that both serve the vulnerable and oppressed and also challenge individuals, organizations, and systems that create oppression and enslavement. These solutions include, but are not limited to prayer, education, rescue, aftercare, proclamation, voting, protest, and an engaged discipleship that sees living justly as integral to spiritual and community formation.

As we minister to all who are touched by modern slavery/human trafficking, we do so with basic underlying convictions:

A. We commit to centering the work of setting captives free on Jesus our redeemer and his mission.

B. We commit to working for holistic freedom. God desires for each person to experience the joy and hope of being free from physical, mental, emotional, and spiritual captivity.

C. We commit to integrating the work of ending modern slavery/human trafficking with both the orthodoxy and orthopraxy of the church. Ending modern slavery/human trafficking is integrally related to ending other injustices. Additionally, hopeful solutions for injustices are found in the community and character formation of people and institutions pursuing holiness.

D. We commit to setting captives free within an atmosphere of worship and community, seeking partnerships with others while embracing lament, humility, prayer, and love.

E. We commit to work towards the mobilization of all influencers within society, knowing that the church on mission with God is the greatest change agent in society.

*For both local and global context the terms "modern slavery" and "human trafficking" are used. Globally, the term human trafficking is more common. In the U.S., and among leading abolitionist organizations, the term modern slavery is widely used. The term "human trafficking" has a specific legal context, but within a church context they are somewhat interchangeable. The term "modern slavery" is stronger for this resolution because of our historical context and because of the reality of the problem.[1]

1) *Book of Discipline* (Indianapolis: Free Methodist Publishing House, 2016), 48-49.

APPENDIX B:

In Ed Stetzer's book, Planting Missional Churches (Nashville: B&H Publishing, 2006), he discusses ten characteristics of a missional church. Notice the balance between evangelism and justice. Consider each of these qualities and rank how well your church or group represents these values from one (not at all) to ten (extremely well):

1. Being unashamedly spiritual
   1 2 3 4 5 6 7 8 9 10

2. Promoting incarnational ministry
   1 2 3 4 5 6 7 8 9 10

3. Engaging in service
   1 2 3 4 5 6 7 8 9 10

4. Valuing experiential praise
   1 2 3 4 5 6 7 8 9 10

5. Preaching narrative expository messages
   1 2 3 4 5 6 7 8 9 10

6. Appreciating and participating in ancient patterns
   1 2 3 4 5 6 7 8 9 10

7. Visualizing worship (not entertainment, but engagement)
   1 2 3 4 5 6 7 8 9 10

8. Connecting with technology (ie: engaging people online)
   1 2 3 4 5 6 7 8 9 10

9. Living in community
1 2 3 4 5 6 7 8 9 10

10. Leading by transparency and team
1 2 3 4 5 6 7 8 9 10

APPENDIX C:

Below are some of the kinds of questions we urge our team leaders to reflect on regularly. You may want to consider using these for your own group or church ministry, ranking yourself from 1 (disagree strongly) to 10 (agree strongly):

1. When we meet, our team prays together and cultivates an environment where each person is inspired to take steps towards spiritual growth.
   1 2 3 4 5 6 7 8 9 10 N/A

2. We foster a spirit of joy, fun, and hope.
   1 2 3 4 5 6 7 8 9 10 N/A

3. Our team intentionally engages members of our community in sharing the hope of Christ with them.
   1 2 3 4 5 6 7 8 9 10 N/A

4. We intentionally place ourselves in situations, gatherings, and places where we can connect with other people for God's purposes.
   1 2 3 4 5 6 7 8 9 10 N/A

5. Our team works well with other groups, agencies, churches, or denominations in our community.
   1 2 3 4 5 6 7 8 9 10 N/A

6. We intentionally listen to other service providers or those we are trying to serve before we assume what they need.
   1 2 3 4 5 6 7 8 9 10 N/A

7. Our group addresses the root causes of issues in our community instead of only examining the symptoms.
   1 2 3 4 5 6 7 8 9 10 N/A

8. We are seeking creative ways to address the harmful value systems that perpetuate injustice and brokenness in our neighborhoods.
   1 2 3 4 5 6 7 8 9 10 N/A

9. We are committed to continual learning and don't assume we have all the answers.
   1 2 3 4 5 6 7 8 9 10 N/A

10. We re-evaluate our process regularly to ensure we are on mission with God.
    1 2 3 4 5 6

Which areas is your church or group doing well? Which areas can you improve? What might those improvements realistically look like?

BIBLIOGRAPHY

For further understanding of freedom, discipleships, and missions issues you might consider reading these:

Bales, Kevin. Disposable People. London: University of California Press, 1999.

------. End Slavery. London: University of California Press, 2007.

------. Understanding Global Slavery. London: University of California Press, 2005.

Batstone, David. Not For Sale. New York: HarperCollins, 2010.

------. "What's the Role of Faith in Fighting Slavery?" CNN. http://thecnnfreedomproject.blogs.cnn.com (February 3, 2012).

Bennetts, Leslie. "The John Next Door." The Daily Beast: http://www.thedailybeast.com (July 17, 2011).

Bergman, Katie. "The Deeper Problems Behind Human Trafficking" Relevantmagazine.com Reject Apathy. (July 14, 2015) http://www.relevantmagazine.com/reject-apathy/deeper-problems-behind-human-trafficking.

------. When Justice Just Is. Bloomington: Westbow Press, 2015.

Block, Peter. Community: The Structure of Belonging. San Francisco: Berrett-Koehler, 2008.

Blow, Charles. "Yes All Men." New York Times, June 1, 2014 http://nyti.ms/SnyqwQ (accessed June 1, 2014).

Brueggemann, Walter. Ichabod Toward Home. Grand Rapids: William B. Eerdmans Publishing, 2002.

------. Biblical Perspectives on Evangelism. Nashville: Abingdon Press, 1993.

------. Finally Comes the Poet. Minneapolis: Fortress Press, 1985.

------. Hopeful Imagination. Philadelphia: Fortress Press, 1986.

------. The Prophetic Imagination. Philadelphia: Fortress Press, 1978.

------. Genesis. Louisville: John Knox Press, 2010.

------. Living Toward a Vision: Biblical Reflections on Shalom. New York: United Church Press, 1982.

------. The Journey to the Common Good. Louisville: Westminster Press, 2010.

Callen, Barry L. and Thorsen, Don. Heart and Life. Aldersgate, 2012.

"Child Sexual Exploitation and Trafficking in Georgia," Interfaith Children's Movement. August, 2009, http://icmma.org/LinkClick.aspx?fileticket=VQhool8eoas%3D&tabid=64 (accessed July 3, 2014).

Christian, Jayakumar. God of the Empty-Handed. Victoria: World Vision: Acorn Press, 1999.

Cho, Eugene. Overrated: Are We More in Love with the Idea of Changing the World than Actually Changing the World? Colorado Springs; David C. Cook, 2014.

Corbett, Steve and Fikkert, Brian. When Helping Hurts. Chicago: Moody, 2009.

Cone, James H. God of the Oppressed. Maryknoll: Orbis Books, 1975.

Crabb, Larry. Becoming a True Spiritual Community. Nashville: Thomas Nelson, 1999.

Crutchfield, Leslie R. and McLeod Grant, Heather. Forces for Good: The Six Practices of High-Impact Nonprofits. San Francisco: Jossey-Bass, 2012.

Free the Slaves: Community Based Model for Fighting Slavery, September 26, 2014, https://www.freetheslaves.net/document.doc?id=355, 2 (accessed December 30, 2014).

Gladwell, Malcolm. Why the Revolution will not be Tweeted. New York: New Yorker Magazine, October 4, 2010 http://www.newyorker.com/reporting/2010/10/04/101004fa_fact_gladwell?currentPage=all.

------. The Tipping Point: How Little Things Can Make a Big Difference. New York: Little, Brown and Company.

Glancy, Jennifer A. Slavery as Moral Problem in the Early Church and Today. Minneapolis: Fortress Press, 2011.

Gordon, Wayne and Perkins, John. Making Neighborhoods Whole: A Handbook for Christian Community Development. Downer's Grove: Intervarsity, 2013.

Grenz, Stanley J., Theology for the Community of God. Grand Rapids: Eerdmans, 1994.

Haugen, Gary. Just Courage. Downer's Grove: Intervarsity Press, 2008.

------. The Locust Effect. New York: Oxford University Press, 2014. Hirsch, Alan and Tim Catchim. The Permanent Revolution. San Francisco: Jossey-Bass, 2012.

------.The Forgotten Ways. Grand Rapids: Brazos Press, 2006.

------. Disciplism. Exponential Resources, 2014.

Hoang, Bethany. Deepening the Soul for Justice. Downer's Grove: InterVarsity, 2012.

Hunter, James Davison, To Change the World: The Irony, Tragedy, and Possibility of Christianity in the Late Modern World. New York: Oxford University Press, 2010.

International Justice Mission: Community Justice Assessment Tool. https://www.ijm.org/sites/default/files/download/resources/Community-Justice-Assessment-Tool.pdf (accessed on February 9, 2015).

Jones, E. Stanley. Christ at the Round Table. New York: Abington Press, 1928.

------. The Unshakeable Kingdom and the Unchanging Person. Nashville: Abingdon, 1972.

Katongole, Emmanuel and Rice, Chris. Reconciling All Things: A Christian Vision for Justice, Peace and Healing (Resources for Reconciliation) 2008.

Kara, Siddharth. Sex Trafficking: Inside the Business of Modern Slavery. New York: Columbia University Press, 2009.

_______. Bonded Labor: Tackling the System of Slavery in South Asia. New York: Columbia University Press, 2009.

King, Martin Luther, Jr. Letter from Birmingham Jail. San Francisco: HarperSanFrancisco, 1963.

------. A Testament of Hope: The Essential Writings of Martin Luther King, Jr. San Francisco: HarperSanFrancisco, 2003.

Kinghorn, Kenneth Cain, ed. John Wesley on the The Sermon on the Mount - The Standard Sermons in Modern English Vol. II, 21-33. Nashville: Abingdon Press, 2002.

------. John Wesley on Christian Practice The Standard Sermons in Modern English Vol. III, 34-53. Nashville: Abingdon Press, 2002.

------. John Wesley on Christian Beliefs The Standard Sermons in Modern English Vol. I, 1-20. Nashville: Abingdon Press, 2002.

Linthicum, Robert. Transforming power: Biblical strategies for making a Difference in your Community. Downers Grove: Intervarsity, 2003.

Maddox Randy L. Responsible Grace. Nashville: Abingdon, 1994.

"Maimonides eight levels of Charity" Chabad.org: http://www.chabad.org/library/article_cdo/aid/45907/jewish/Eight-Levels-of-Charity.htm (accessed December 26, 2014).

Mannoia, Kevin W. and Thosen, Don, eds. The Holiness Manifesto. Grand Rapids: Eerdmans, 2008.

Marsh, Charles. The Beloved Community. New York: Basic Books, 2005.

Martin, Jim. The Just Church: Becoming a Risk-Taking, Justice-Seeking, Disciple-Making Congregation. Chicago: Tyndale House Kindle Edition.

McKnight, John and Block, Peter. The Abundant Community: Awakening the power of families and neighborhoods. San Francisco: Berrett-Koehler, 2010.

Myers, Bryant L. Walking With The Poor: Principles and Practices of Transformational Development. Maryknoll: Orbis Books, 2011, Kindle Edition.

Park, Madison "WHO: 1 in 3 women experience physical or sexual violence", CNN, June 20, 2013. http://www.cnn.com/2013/06/20/health/global-violence-women/ (accessed May 26, 2014).

Perkins, John. With Justice for All. Ventura: Regal Books, 1982.

------. and Charles Marsh Welcoming Justice: God's Movement Toward Beloved Community (Resources for Reconciliation). Downers Grove: InterVarsity Press, Kindle Edition, 2009.

Putnam, Robert. Bowling Alone. New York: Simon and Schuster, 2000.

______. and Feldstein, Lewis M. Better Together. New York: Simon and Schuster, 2003.

Radner, Ephraim. Leviticus. Grand Rapids: Brazos Press, 2008.

Ringe, Sharon. Jesus, Liberation, and the Biblical Jubilee. Philadelphia: Fortress Press, 1985.

Sacks, Rabbi Jonathan. To Heal a Fractured World. New York: Schocken Books, 2005.

Set Free Movement, Set Free Primer. http://www.setfreemovement.org/hp_wordpress/wp-content/uploads/2013/07/Set-Free-Primer.pdf

------. Case Statement. http://setfreemovement.com/wp-content/uploads/2013/12/SFM-Case-Statement.pdf

Skinner, Benjamin. A Crime so Monstrous. New York: Free Press, 2008.

Snyder, Howard. The Community of the King. Downers Grove: Intervarsity Press, 2nd edition, 2004.

------. The Radical Wesley. Downers Grove: Inter-varsity Press, 1980.

------, B.T. and Ellen Roberts and the First Free Methodists, Abridged Edition of Populist Saints: B.T. and Ellen Roberts and the Early Free Methodists, by Daniel V. Runyon. Indianapolis: Committee on Free Methodist History and Archives
Marston Memorial Historical Center, 2011.

------ and Joel Scandrett, Salvation Means Creation Healed: The Ecology of Sin and Grace: Overcoming the Divorce Between Earth and Heaven. Eugene: Cascade Books, 2011.

Sorajjakool, Siroj. Child Prostitution in Thailand, Listening to Rahab. New York: Haworth Press, 2003.

Strickland, Danielle. "Social Evils the Army has Challenged" Armybarmy http://www.armybarmy.com/JAC/article2-63.html (accessed July 21, 2015.).

Theocharous, Myrto. "Stealing Souls: Human Trafficking and Deuteronomy 24:7" from For Our God Always: Studies on the Message and Influence of Deuteronomy in Honor of David I. Block. DeRouchie, Jason Gile, and Kenneth J. Turner, eds. Winona Lake: Eisenbrauns, 2013.

Thurman, Howard. Jesus and the Disinherited Boston: Beacon, 1976.

Walk Free Foundation: Global Slavery Index. http://www.globalslaveryindex.org (accessed October 21, 2014).

Walzer, Michael. Exodus and Revolution. New York: Basic Books, 1985.

Ware, Bishop Kallistos. The Orthodox Way. Crestwood: St. Vladimir's Seminary Press, 1979.

Weld, Theodore. The Bible against slavery: an inquiry into the patriarchal and Mosaic systems on the subject of human rights. New York: American Anti-Slavery Society, 1838.

Wilberforce, William. Real Christianity. Ventura: Regal Books, 2006.

Willimon, William H. and Hawerwas, Stanley. Resident Aliens: Life in the Christian Colony. Expanded 25th Anniversary Edition. Nashville: Abingdon Press, 2014.

Willard, Dallas. Renovation of the Heart. Colorado Springs: Navpress, 2002.

------. The Divine Conspiracy. San Francisco: HarperSanFrancisco, 1998.

Woodward, J.R. Creating a Missional Culture. Downers Grove: Intervarsity Press, 2012.

Wright, Christopher J.H. The Mission of God. Downers Grove: IVP Academy, 2006.

Wytsma, Ken. Pursuing Justice. Nashville: Thomas Nelson. 2013.

FINAL THOUGHT

Knowing God is the highest priority of humanity, because knowing God changes us. We hope that this issue has given you a fresh perspective and equipped you with the raw materials God can use to keep you learning the Way of Jesus.

Sincerely,
Dr. David McDonald
Editor, FreeMo Journals

DISCIPLE DEEPLY

BY DR. DAVID MCDONALD WITH MARK VAN VALIN

The original twelve disciples were thickheaded, ego-driven, and blind; so, clearly, you don't have to be perfect in order to follow Jesus. But it seems like we give ourselves too much leeway to behave poorly, to think sloppily, or to interact disingenuously. Because "nobody's perfect" we don't put a lot of effort into the process of our ongoing perfection.

We ought to change that.

EMBRACE ALL

BY JOANNA DEWOLF

The best stories only get better over time and nothing captures our hearts like the story of Jesus' birth.

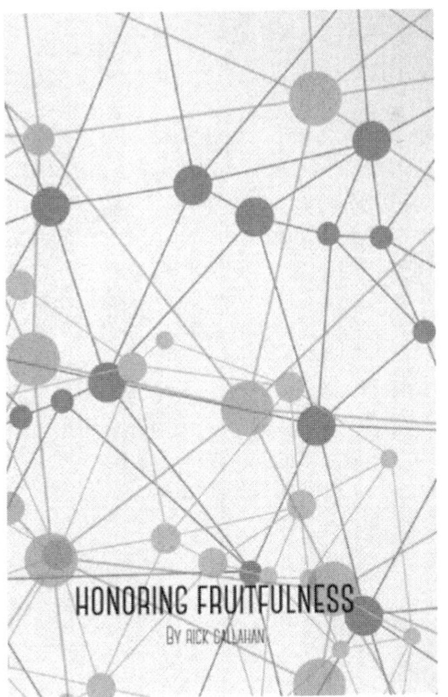

HONORING FRUITFULNESS

BY RICK CALLAHAN

Jesus offers an abundant life–a life that is deep and wide, full of meaning and purpose.

CULTIVATING HEALTH

BY CHERYL WAYMAN

Why is it so hard to heal our broken relationships? How can God transform not only our relationships but our emotions as well?

PARTNER STRONG
BY BEN REDMOND

Partnership is not an optional endeavor for those of us who follow Jesus. God has placed us in this exact moment of human history, and He has chosen us as His partners. Not based on our resume or talent. No, God picks His partners based on availability over ability.

So now it's our turn to partner with God, with each other, and with the world as we find our place in the greatest story of them all.

MULTIPLY MINISTRIES
BY LARRY WALKEMEYER

Mustard plants are one of the most remarkable plants in God's garden. As a spice, mustard is only surpassed in importance by salt and pepper. It is one of the hardiest and most generative herbs. Mustard multiplies.

As followers of Jesus we are often tempted to look in the mirror at our own limited dimensions and envision the future based on the reflection we see. What can I do? How much can my ministry accomplish? How can our little church have an impact?
How can we leave a significant legacy?

The answer?

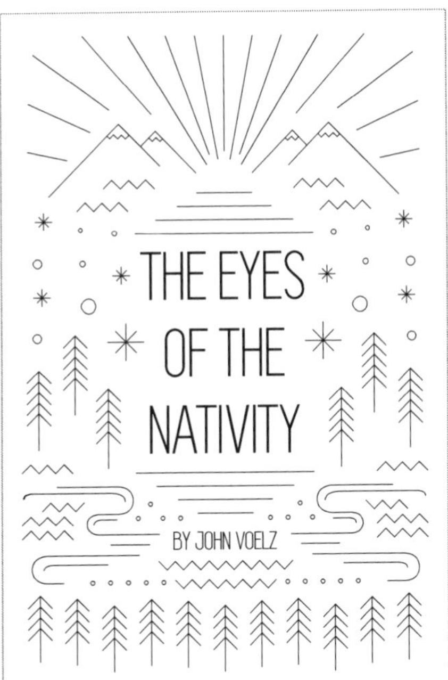

THE EYES OF THE NATIVITY
BY JOHN VOELZ

There are stories we casually enjoy and then there are stories that compel us to act. This book has 13 chapters about the nativity. Each one looks at the nativity through different eyes–different stages of life, different responsibilities and roles.

It's easy to fall in the trap of telling the Christmas narrative with the enthusiasm of someone reciting Hickory Dickory Dock. But, if we pay attention, the nativity will propel us to follow Christ confidently not as though he were far away, but because we know him as Immanuel: God with us.

SHADOWING GOD
BY DAVID MCDONALD

God wants to do more in us
and through us than for us and to us.

God's ways are subtle, and they are all around us, but we don't often perceive him or his work in the world because we are looking for something clumsy and big to show us our destiny.

We must learn to see God's activity in the world just behind the one we see, in the shadows, toward the wings, and just off-stage.

But once we pay attention to what's happening just behind everything we see with our eyes, we are introduced to another world, to a better world, and a better life in it.

DEVELOPING LEADERS
BY DR. ROB MCKENNA

Incarnational leaders and disciples have something in common - a desire to follow Jesus.

The path to growth has less to do with ascension and upward movement. The path to growth always starts with a sacrifice.

This book is designed to cultivate your character, an essential component of both Christian discipleship and leadership. You can use this material to make disciples in your church, at work, and in your family. How is this possible? Again, both leadership and discipleship are dependent upon faithfully following Jesus, so the emphasis of this book is on the formation of Christ-like character.

The FreeMo Journal is published 5 times each year (Fall, Christmas, January, Easter, and Summer). Subscriptions are available through Light + Life Communication and previous issues can be ordered from The Wesleyan Publishing House at (800) 493.7539.

IF YOU'RE INTERESTED IN WRITING FOR THE FREEMO JOURNAL,